feng shui
guide to
harmonious
living

feng shui
guide to
harmonious
living

101 ways to clear life's clutter

mary lambert

CICO BOOKS
London

Published by Cico Books Ltd
32 Great Sutton Street
London EC1V 0NB

This edition published in 2003. *Feng Shui Guide to Harmonious Living*
was previously published in 2002 exclusively for Book Club Associates as
Clearing the Clutter Book of Purification.

10 9 8 7 6 5 4 3 2 1

A CIP catalogue record for this book is available from the British Library

ISBN 1-903116-53-8

All photography by Geoff Dann, except:
Page 7 Andrew Wood
Page 11 Andrew Wood/Babylon Design, courtesy of
    the Interior Archive, London
Page 66 Gloria Nicol

Editor: Mandy Greenfield
Design: Sara Kidd
Cover design: David Fordham
Illustrations:
    Joan Corlass (pp 13, 15, 17, 21, 25, 29, 33, 37, 41, 45,
        50–51, 61, 62, 71, 72–73, 75, 76, 79, 81, 83, 84, 87)
    Moira Wills (pp 8, 10, 18, 22, 26, 30, 34, 38, 42, 46, 48, 63)
    Samantha Wilson (pp 16, 20, 24, 28, 32, 36, 40, 44, 85)
    Kate Simunek (p 59)
Line art: Stephen Dew

Contents

Introduction

Clutter is a modern phenomenon. In today's world we basically have too many possessions, and because we form such a strong emotional attachment to things that we own, letting go of them becomes a major issue. But holding on to clutter is not good for you. In feng shui, the Chinese art of furniture placement and energy flow, it is believed that for us to live happily and healthily in our homes, energy (or chi) has to be able to flow through each room in a smooth, spiral pattern. When large piles of clutter build up in your home, the path of this energy becomes blocked, so the flow slows down or becomes erratic. This in turn affects the people living there, to the extent that when there is clutter overload, they can feel that they are completely stymied and unable to make any real progress in their lives.

MAKING CHANGE

The aim of this book is to give you the tools to start the process of clearing out, learning how to purify your home's energy and move on to new and better opportunities. The first part of the book explains how you can place the Pa Kua, a valuable feng shui diagnostic tool, over a plan of the rooms in your house or apartment to find out where your eight aspirational areas are (see pages 12–15). These are highly influential, because they reflect important aspects of our lives: Career, Wealth and Prosperity, Marriage and Romantic Happiness, Recognition and Fame, Children and New Beginnings, Education and Knowledge, Mentors and Networking, and Family and Health. If you have let clutter gather in these areas, you will be suffering from the aftereffects – your children may have become disruptive, romantic relationships may be hard work or simply not happening, or perhaps you don't seem to be getting anywhere in your career. Removing these unwanted items, or giving them to other people, using the five-bag system (see pages 48–51), will transform your life for the better.

CLEANSING THE ATMOSPHERE

The second part of the book is about purification. When your clutter has been removed, you may still be left with a very sluggish, stale ambience that needs a definite kickstart. Purifying – using techniques such as smudging with smoking herbs, misting with fragrant aromatherapy oils, and using the humming sound of singing bowls – can give you back a vibrancy in the atmosphere that you may not have thought possible. Different

ceremonies can be performed to shift the stale energy, some of which are more powerful than others. But the choice is yours, and you will intuitively feel which is the right one for you.

You can also create your own special ceremonies (see pages 88–93) to support areas of your life that may require further attention.

A pure space
Clearing clutter and purifying your space removes stagnancy and brings liberation and energy.

Reclaiming your home from its clutter is liberating, and cleansing it of any residual stagnancy makes you feel free to do new things and to live life to the full.

Making Your Home Work for You

Clutter can be insidious: once a pile of it forms it seems to generate another, and before you know it, it has taken over. You slow down, and so does anyone else living with you; any change in routine becomes terrifying. You want to get rid of junk, but it

seems to be controlling you, dictating that your life is going nowhere at the moment.

Having a clearout, even if you only begin with a single drawer, starts you on the path to letting go of belongings that you no longer need. It breaks the clutter-building cycle; it stops the process that has been draining your energy and preventing you from moving forward.

Use the questionnaire opposite to find out if you are suffering from clutter overload. Answer the questions to work out how much clutter has gathered in different areas of your home. Score two points for "guilty," one for "not so guilty," and zero for "innocent."

YOUR SCORE

30–40 You have a serious clutter problem. Schedule your clearout now.
20–30 Clutter is starting to pile up, so get to grips with it now, and throw or give away anything you don't need.
10–20 You have some clutter, but not much; get rid of it and keep it that way.
Under 10 Be proud of yourself, for you are not a hoarder. But don't get complacent.

Clutter magnets
The telephone and computer are natural clutter magnets that attract items no longer needed.

IS YOUR LIFE FULL OF CLUTTER?

**Guilty Not so Innocent
guilty**

1 The hall There are bikes, broken umbrellas, golf clubs, dirty shoes, and newspapers blocking the door.

2 You knock off coats and jackets from the bulging coatstand as you come in.

3 The living room The TV unit is bulging with old videos, unreturned DVDs, and old tapes.

4 The bookshelves are crammed with books you haven't looked at for a year.

5 The coffee table or magazine rack is full of periodicals or newspapers to be recycled.

6 The bedroom You have a closet full of clothes, some of which don't fit you, and you wear only a fraction of them.

7 There are shoes everywhere, even ones with broken heels, but you only like three or four pairs.

8 The children's bedrooms The rooms are like a skating rink when you walk in, because of all the toys underfoot.

9 There are still baby clothes and garments that have been outgrown in your youngster's room.

10 Old storybooks, jigsaws, and forgotten computer games are stacked in corners.

11 The bathroom Old medicines, skin creams, broken razors, and tired toothbrushes line your cabinets.

12 You can't actually climb in the bath because it is ringed with half-finished bath oils, lotions, shampoos, and soaps.

13 Free samples of moisturizer, cleansers, toners, and other items are falling out of your storage units.

14 The kitchen Spices, packages of food, and cans have been in your kitchen cabinets, unused, for months.

15 The home office The floor is littered with files and papers, and you can never find anything.

16 Newspaper clippings, notes, reminders, and bills line your desk.

17 Your computer has so many files you can never locate anything – you rarely delete your emails.

18 The attic This is so full of junk you are afraid to venture up there.

19 All your past is kept there – old children's toys, sports gear, piles of romantic and school memorabilia.

20 The garage It's so crammed with clutter that you can't get the car in and have to leave it outside.

TOTAL SCORE

Working out your aims

Now you need to be strict with yourself and work out what you want to achieve with your clutter-clearing. If you know that a certain part of your life (say, your health) has been suffering recently, then map out your home or your rooms (see pages 12–15) and see if your Family and Health areas are loaded with clutter. Otherwise, make a plan of action, go around each room with a notepad, and write down all the problem areas, highlighting the worst spots that need to be tackled first. Then set yourself a timescale for dealing with them. Make your clearing-out goals immediate, short-term, and long-term, writing timings against each one. An immediate goal might be simply to empty the trashcan in the kitchen. Be realistic – if you have a serious amount of junk in every room, it could take you months!

TOP FIVE CLUTTER MOUNTAINS

Clutter gathers everywhere in the home, but there are certain places that seem to be particular culprits, or where clutter is detrimental to the beneficial flow of energy (chi).

♦ **Behind doors** Storing clutter here prevents the door opening properly and hinders energy from entering the home or room easily.

Watch out for: (bedroom) piles of dirty

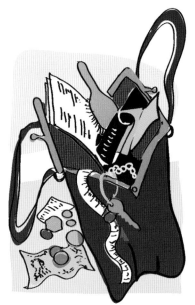

Dealing with overload
A bulging bag crammed with outdated receipts, keys, and paperwork creates negative energy.

clothes, overflowing laundry basket; (kitchen) full trashcan, piles of newspapers.

♦ **On or down the side of closets** These lurking clutter piles weigh down on us, creating a heavy presence that can literally give us a headache.

Watch out for: dented suitcases, old bed linen that is never used, battered or unwanted handbags, scarves, unworn hats, boxes of junk, unwanted presents.

♦ **Inside closets** "Too many clothes, but nothing to wear" is the cry of many women. Men also hang on to old clothes that they don't wear any more. As your energy changes, so does your taste in clothes, so throw or give away any items that no longer fit you or that you haven't worn for a year.

Watch out for: sexy or trendy shoes that just don't fit, wornout sneakers, too-tight pants, skirts, and jackets, garish sweaters, dated power-suits, old ties, shirts with fraying collars.

♦ **Under beds** This is a veritable dumping ground, but don't think that because you can't see the clutter, you can forget about it. In adult bedrooms this stagnant presence can affect your love life; in a child's bedroom it can cause restless sleep.

Watch out for: (in an adult's room) old periodicals, discarded self-help or sex books, tissues, broken clocks, torn pantyhose, socks with holes, broken hairdryers; (in a child's room) broken toys, torn books, one-armed teddy bears, and lost school books.

♦ **On the floor** If you are always weaving your way through junk scattered around your hall, living room, kitchen, or other rooms, no wonder life feels such a struggle. Chi needs to meander, not stop and start around miscellaneous paraphernalia.

Watch out for: (hallway) junk mail, boxes, newspapers, auto parts, old boots, and piles of paperwork on the stairs; (kitchen) bottles and old cartons.

Office clutter

Your office at work, and particularly home offices, are often storehouses of clutter, from old faxes to disused files and unused computer disks. Keep the area around the desk junk-free for good energy flow.

From Clutter to Clarity

Before you perform a purification ceremony (see pages 52–93), you need to work out what effect your clutter is having on you. Junk mountains festering in the eight aspirational areas of your home and life will only hamper your progress and sap your vitality. So de-clutter these special spaces now – and turn negative clutter into the positive energy of harmony and opportunity.

USING THE PA KUA TO SET YOUR GOALS

To discover where your aspirational areas are you need to use the Pa Kua. This ancient octagonal figure with six rings is an essential diagnostic feng shui tool, which is used by consultants to map out the vibrational energy of a home. Each of its eight aspirational areas corresponds to a direction of the compass and reflects an important part of your life:

♦ **South** represents Recognition and Fame – your inherent talent, how you are seen in the world.

♦ **Southwest** stands for Marriage and Romantic Happiness – your loving relationship with that special partner.

♦ **West** symbolizes Children and New Beginnings – your descendants, bundles of joy and hope, and new aspirations for the future.

♦ **Northwest** signifies Mentors and Networking – the people who guide you or help you get on in life.

♦ **North** represents Career – your work ambitions and success in business.

♦ **Northeast** stands for Education and Knowledge – your potential for further study and achievement.

♦ **East** symbolizes Family and Health – you and your family's good health and wellbeing.

♦ **Southeast** represents Wealth and Prosperity – the family's money prospects and other things that are important to them.

The Pa Kua shows how all the energy (chi) moves within these spaces. Where there are cluttered areas, that energy will be negative and slow; where there are bare spaces, it will be slightly stagnant. Using the Pa Kua gives you a special way of looking at your home as an expression of your life.

Don't forget that your home acts as a mirror, reflecting what is (or is not) going on in your life at the moment. Once you have placed a copy of the Pa Kua over a plan of your home or rooms, it will reveal exactly what is happening to you at the present time. So if you are mentally saying to yourself, "I feel trapped", "My way forward seems blocked", or "I feel empty inside", look around your home and see where these feelings are being physically expressed. You may originally have created a clutter situation as a means of self-protection, but now feel ready to shift the energy and bring about change. These are obviously priority areas to work on. Make a list on where you are going to start in your home, and give yourself a timescale in which to sort these spaces out.

The Pa Kua sectors

The Pa Kua features an inner ring containing the trigrams, and a number of outer rings, which include the five elements – Wood, Metal, Earth, Fire, and Water that align with each trigram and compass direction.

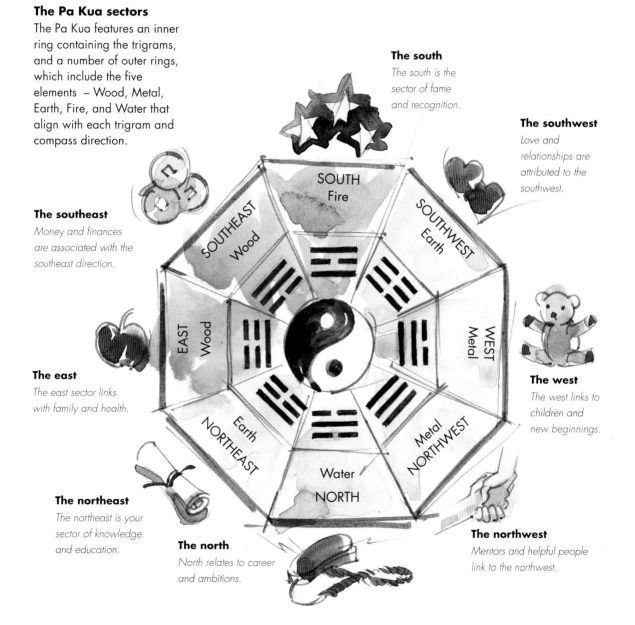

The south
The south is the sector of fame and recognition.

The southwest
Love and relationships are attributed to the southwest.

The southeast
Money and finances are associated with the southeast direction.

The east
The east sector links with family and health.

The west
The west links to children and new beginnings.

The northeast
The northeast is your sector of knowledge and education.

The north
North relates to career and ambitions.

The northwest
Mentors and helpful people link to the northwest.

SOUTH
Fire

SOUTHEAST
Wood

SOUTHWEST
Earth

EAST
Wood

WEST
Metal

NORTHEAST
Earth

Water
NORTH

Metal
NORTHWEST

Room for change

Placing the Pa Kua over each room plan, rather than a plan of your whole house or apartment, will pinpoint more clearly where major clutter problems exist (see the instructions shown opposite). You will find a surprising link between areas of your life you are struggling with, and junk in these aspirational areas of your home. For example, if you discover that there is a mountain of broken items, piles of unwanted clothes, shoes, and discarded makeup under your bed in the Marriage and Romantic Happiness area of your bedroom, then you may start to realize why your relationship has been in the doldrums recently. If one of your Wealth areas is dull, dusty, and contains a photograph of a depressed-looking person, piles of bills, broken electrical equipment, an empty cash box, and other assorted junk, then you may start to understand why your bank account has not exactly been florishing.

Is your home office used as a dump? Is it a struggle to get through the door and walk to your computer because of heaps of junk mail, bundles of old letters, and disused files that have taken root there? If so, your career is not going to prosper. It is essential to discover where your negative areas are so that you can clear them out, energize them, and move on to better things in your life.

PURITY POINT 1

♦ If you are single, dull, negative energy in your love sector could prevent you finding that special new person in your life. De-junking and purifying this area can bring you new love.

Sea change
Natural sea salt is an ancient remedy for stagnant energy, and it is one of the simplest purifiers available. It absorbs residual negative energy that can linger after a de-junking session.

MAPPING OUT YOUR HOME

To find out where your clutter is gathering, first take your home's directions so that you can use the Pa Kua. It is best to map out each room individually, rather than putting the Pa Kua over a plan of your whole home.

♦ With an orienteering compass in your hand, stand in your hall facing the front door to check which direction the energy comes in from. Make sure the north pointer (often red) aligns with north as you do this. So if the north pointer is facing to the right, then the energy straight ahead is coming from the west.

♦ Go around each room with your compass, standing in the doorway looking outward, and note down the direction the room faces.

♦ Draw a rough sketch of each room, showing the doorway, its direction, and any basic furniture on graph paper.

♦ Place a copy of the Pa Kua (you can xerox the one on page 96) over the room, matching up the door's directions. If the room energy comes from the south, place the Recognition and Fame sector right on the doorway and mark in the other seven areas.

♦ If a room is an odd shape and part of an aspirational area seems to be missing, don't worry. You can bring this empty space back in by placing mirrors, lights, or houseplants on or next to the internal wall to stimulate the energy there.

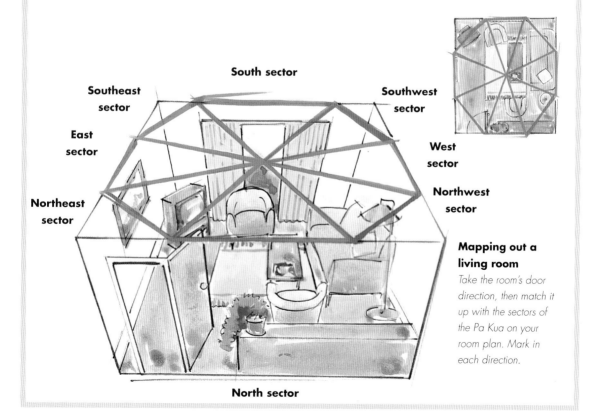

South sector

Southeast sector

Southwest sector

East sector

West sector

Northeast sector

Northwest sector

North sector

Mapping out a living room

Take the room's door direction, then match it up with the sectors of the Pa Kua on your room plan. Mark in each direction.

Getting Star Quality

Your Recognition and Fame area is in the south of your home, or the south of each room. It represents the Fire element, the heat of summer, the inspiring warmth that comes from the midday sun, and vibrant yang energy. Fire's heat and brightness give this area a strong, almost explosive quality. It deals with recognition: how people perceive you, your individuality, your talents and achievements. It is about your reputation, clarity, charisma, and vision. Spiritually, it concerns your understanding of the world and how enlightened you are.

REAL-LIFE FAME

A client whom I visited worked as a nutritional therapist, and when I went to see her she was moaning that she wasn't getting enough patients. On mapping out the flat, I found her framed diploma discarded behind the sofa, so she was hiding all her skill and talent. I moved it to her Fame area. A few days later old patients got in touch and new ones started ringing her.

Getting noticed

To bring more star vibrations into your life, or to be seen by other people as happy and successful, you need to de-clutter your Fame area.

ALL CLUTTERED UP

So what happens if you discover that your Fame area is full of clutter? Think back over the last few months – has life seemed a constant struggle, with nobody really paying any attention to you? Have you argued or fallen out with friends, or received fewer social invitations than usual? Have you been passed over for promotion at work? If your Fame area is giving off negative energy, it is like a veil being drawn over you – your talents start to become invisible to the world.

RECOGNITION CHECKLIST

Ask yourself the following questions about your recognition: how people are seeing you and reacting to you. If you answer "Yes" to any, investigate your Fame areas for hidden junk. If so, remove it straight away, purify the area, and see how you become visible once more.

♦ Are you failing to get the recognition you deserve for the work you do?

♦ Do you feel your friends aren't listening to your opinions and seem to criticize you?

♦ If you are in the public eye (a writer or an actor), do you always get bad reviews?

♦ Have you placed an advertisement relating to your talents, but received no replies?

♦ If you regularly do presentations or talks, do you feel that people seem to lack interest in what you are saying?

♦ Are you normally the life and soul of the party, but now try to avoid social gatherings?

ACTION PLAN

Have a serious look at your Fame area(s) and at its contents. Throw away any general junk, such as broken items, old newspapers, or ornaments that you dislike. Then look carefully at what is left. Check if there are too many items that are connected to the old "you" and not the new "you" that you aspire to.  Remove items such as framed photographs of you at your graduation, or any photographs in which you look unhappy, along with cards from friends whom you no longer see. Objects such as these connect you to energy from a past life – and you are a different person now.

Get rid of critical letters and job rejections, as these project failure. If you receive reviews in your chosen profession, dispose of any bad ones, because these are implying that you will never be a success. Dried flowers or dying plants also give out negative energy, so remove these. If you are a musician, but have stored an instrument in your Fame area(s) that you never play, sell it or give it away to someone who will use it.

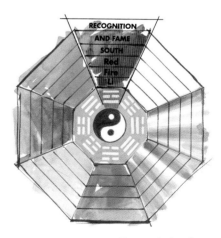

Fame is in the south
Your Fame area links to red, the Fire element, and the trigram Li.

Getting positive

You need to create an area that feeds in positive energy, stimulating your uniqueness, embracing the person you are now and the person you want to be. Remember that we react very strongly to symbolism, so including images in your Fame area of the way you see yourself (or what you are trying to attain) can only have a good influence on you.

Think about what makes you feel good about yourself – then add in a photograph of you looking healthy and happy, within a red or wooden frame to support the Fire energy. Place loving or congratulatory cards from friends here to boost your self-esteem. Include any trophies relating to a sport that you currently do well, as this will show that you are a winner. Letters

Fame loser
Loads of trash, old graduation pictures and cards from friends no longer seen send out stagnant vibrations from you Recognition and Fame space. Tarnished trophies, bad reviews, and unused musical instruments promote a bad personal image.

USING INCENSE FOR STARDOM

After clearing out, choose an incense that you are drawn to whose aroma makes you feel good. Light it in a holder, then fan the smoke all around your Fame area, closing your eyes and saying mentally, "I am clearing out old energy and letting myself shine once again." Focus on this for several minutes, then put the incense down and leave it to burn out safely. Burn incense again if your star starts to fade.

confirming a promotion at work or cuttings about a character-building course that you want to undertake will project you in a positive sense. If you are longing for a new car, include an image or toy of the type you really want to buy. Lock into any good emanations coming from newspaper or periodical reviews or clippings that praise your abilities as a performer, writer, or artist. Place any awards that you have received in this area; if you act, positioning a mock Oscar statuette in this space says success – big time.

KEY TO FAME AREA

1 Flowers or plants bring growth and Wood energy.

2 Candles feed the existing Fire energy here.

3 Congratulatory cards or ones from friends emphasize your positive presence in the world.

4 A framed diploma of your profession increases your fame.

5 A model of a desired object, such as a sportscar, can be put here to look at regularly.

6 A framed picture of you looking happy and healthy enhances your image.

7 Placing your published books here, if you are a writer, promotes author recognition.

PURITY POINTS 2–7

THREE OF THE BEST
- ◆ Framed diplomas
- ◆ Desired items
- ◆ A positive photograph of you

THREE OF THE WORST
- ◆ Graduation and school pictures
- ◆ Dying plants and flowers
- ◆ Bad reviews, critical letters

PURITY POINTS 8–11

- ◆ Keep some candles in this area and light them regularly. You can also add some round, red lamps.
- ◆ Place energizing wooden frames, bowls, or ornaments in this area (because in feng shui, Wood feeds Fire in the Productive Cycle of elements).
- ◆ Hang a lead-facetted crystal with red string in the window, to bring in positive yang sun energy.
- ◆ Introduce some healthy round-leaved plants or flowers.

Fame winner
When your clutter is removed from here, increase your fame appeal by tapping into the positive energies of this south corner. Put in symbolic desired images, diplomas, praising cards, good newspaper cuttings or reviews to show how you want to be seen by friends and colleagues.

Enhancing Your Love Life

Your Marriage and Romantic Happiness area is in the southwest of your home or of each room. It represents the Earth element, dependency, and long warm summer days with ripe crops just about to be harvested. This is your corner of love and relationships, where existing relationships with a partner can be cherished and nourished, and where (if you are single) new ones can be encouraged to form. It is the area of passion and sexuality, where you create that strong bond with another person who can make your life so worthwhile. It is about togetherness – a meeting of minds and emotions; in fact, a true blending of the forces of yin and yang.

ALL CLUTTERED UP

If this area has become a clutter haven, what are the effects going to be? Think about how your relationship has been faring recently. Have you and your partner been arguing constantly? Have you lost the desire for loving embraces or

Boosting love

If you want to meet a soul mate or work on improving your present relationship – to stop arguments and improve your sex life – begin by de-junking the Marriage area of your home.

sex, felt tired, and lacked interest in your lover? If you're single, think about whether it has been difficult to meet people in the last few months – or have you found that you meet someone you really like, but after a few dates don't hear from them any more? If dull, stagnant energy is coming from your relationship areas, it means that all the loving vibrations you normally give off are tainted and nothing will seem to work romantically.

ACTION PLAN

Check out your Marriage and Romantic Happiness area(s) to see if there is any clutter

ROMANTIC CHECKLIST

Ask yourself the following questions about your love life. If you answer "Yes" to any, check your romantic areas for clutter immediately. If you find junk or negative items there, clear them out, purify the space, and notice how good things start to happen.

♦ Do you find that you are constantly arguing with your partner?

♦ Is your ex-lover always ringing you, but being nasty and critical and affecting your self-esteem?

♦ Are you experiencing any problems with your sex life?

♦ Do you feel unhappy in your relationship, or do you feel something is not quite right at the moment?

♦ Has your social life plummeted recently, with friends with whom you were once sociable rarely asking you out?

♦ If you're single, is it a long time since you have been out on a hot date?

there, particularly in the bedroom – your most loving room. First, look under the bed and on top of closets, searching out and discarding any unused articles, broken appliances, unworn clothes, ancient shoes, old photographs or books. Now see what other possessions you are storing in the bedroom. Are there things that are making your love life go sour? Or ones that connect you to past

relationships? Remove any old love letters or photographs of previous partners. Check all the pictures that are hanging there and discard any of people who are crying or looking depressed, or any imagery that depicts despair or suggests a broken heart.

REAL-LIFE LOVE

Look carefully in your Marriage and Romantic Happiness area for any pictures of women on their own, if you're female (or men, if you're male) as you need to balance male and female art. A friend of mine had many pictures of pre-Raphaelite women in her flat and her love corners. The paintings were beautiful, but the women looked unhappy and the message she was giving out strongly was that she wasn't happy with her life, and wanted to stay single.

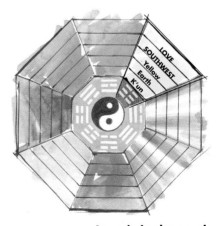

Love is in the southwest
Your Love area links to yellow, the Earth element, and the trigram K'un.

Getting positive

Now you need to make a space that leaves the past behind and emits positive, loving energy to embrace your current relationship, or to pull in the new one that your heart really desires. Remember that you can achieve anything you want to – you just need to project what you desire and the Universe will hear your message.

A good way of fostering this positive energy is to display romantic symbols. Make a love shrine with male and female paired items, such as mandarin ducks or other animals, dolls, or a ceramic statue of a loving couple. Fresh red flowers or red candles can energize the southwest corner of your living room (but no flowers in the bedroom because they are too yang). If you know someone whom you would like as a future partner, put a picture of him or her in this area. And write a list of your potential lover's qualities (but make sure you say whether they should be male or female, as you always get what you ask for!). Be specific in your requests, but in another column include some less appealing aspects of their personality that you would be prepared to accept. Put the list in a box with a chunk of rose quartz – the lover's stone.

Love loser
Clutter everywhere, gungy cosmetics, pictures of old boyfriends, you alone, or broken love ornaments do not foster good love vibes in your Marriage and Romantic happiness space. Ancient love letters or an old engagement ring tie you to past relationships, not allowing a new one to enter.

PURITY POINTS 12–16

♦ Display the Chinese double-happiness symbol here, for extra joy and love.
♦ Use ceramic bowls and ornaments to support the Earth energy.
♦ Include heart-shaped boxes or pictures to symbolize love.
♦ Shine spotlights or uplighters on the corner in question to encourage more romance (Fire feeds Earth).
♦ Hang a two- or nine-rod ceramic windchime here to make you more popular.

PURITY POINTS 17-22

THREE OF THE BEST	THREE OF THE WORST
◆ Male and female paired ornaments	◆ Old love letters
◆ Symbolic picture of future lover	◆ Broken romantic statues
◆ Red energizing candles	◆ Pictures of past partners

KEY TO LOVE AREA

1 A magazine image can depict the new lover that you want to draw in.

2 A paired statue or loving couple photograph encourages romance.

3 A rose quartz crystal, the lover's stone, is good to place here.

4 A pair of red glass hearts emphasizes a loving attachment.

5 Red candles bring boosting Fire energy.

6 Pink tulips or other flowers increase romantic flavor.

Love winner

With your love space cleared, accelerate your romantic outlook in your southwest corner. Place a symbolic lover picture here, paired items, red candles, a potential lover list, and a loving crystal to bring in the partner you desire.

LIFTING THE LOVE VIBE

After clearing out your Marriage and Romantic Happiness area, cleanse it by filling a glass atomizer with water and a few drops of lavender essential oil. Spray around the area to remove any negativity, and make a wish concerning your hopes. Then, in an oil burner, burn some ylang-ylang and geranium essential oil in water, to create a sensuous space. Think, "I am allowing loving feelings into my life." Burn these oils often to lift your love vibrations.

Topping Up Your Wealth

The southeast of your home, or of each room, is the area of your finances. It represents the Wood element, all growing things, and springtime. This is your Wealth and Prosperity area, where seeds are planted for your future fortune. It is about financial success in business, and the security and happiness that you can attain for you and your family. But not everyone is destined to be a millionaire, so this area is also about abundance – it may be in your karma that you are not destined to have lots of money, but just look at all those other important aspects of your life: your fun-filled social life, cherished friends, adored pets, and opportunities that may come your way.

REAL-LIFE WEALTH

Recently I went to the house of a client who had just moved. She was still getting rid of the clutter she had brought with her, and in her bedroom's Wealth area we found an uneven pile of storage boxes full of items she didn't want. I told her to remove them immediately, and instead create an inviting wealth table. The negative wealth energy hadn't affected her yet, but in a few months it would have done.

Boosting wealth

Removing your clutter from your Wealth area frees up your prosperity luck, so abundance and new financial opportunities can flow into your life.

ALL CLUTTERED UP

Investigate whether any clutter you have unknowingly stored in your Wealth area is having a severe effect on your finances. Sit down for a moment and think about your bank account over the last few months. Have you earned money, but then let it slip through your fingers? Are you constantly overspending, and struggling to keep up with your financial commitments? Have you been due a salary increase that was suddenly refused? If, without you being aware of it, your Wealth area is giving off negative emanations, it may mean that your financial acumen is disturbed and your ability to handle money well has become unbalanced or distorted.

PROSPERITY CHECKLIST

Ask yourself the following questions about your financial affairs. If you answer "Yes" to any, then look around your wealth areas and see if they are full of clutter. If you find unwanted items there, get rid of them, do a purification ceremony, and see how quickly your money situation starts to improve.

♦ Have you been getting more in debt in the last few months?

♦ Has your bank refused to increase your spending?

♦ Are your bills becoming unmanageable?

♦ Are you having problems getting a mortgage?

♦ Does your partner keep accusing you of spending too much money?

♦ Have you been told there is no salary increase this year?

ACTION PLAN

Look at your Wealth space(s) and see what clutter is gathering there. Throw or give away anything you don't need: broken appliances, unread books, disused games, and disliked photographs. Separate yourself from your emotions and analyze whether you are keeping things in this area that may be holding you back from having more good fortune.

Work out the symbolic meaning of what you are keeping here. Is there anything linking you to money problems in the past, or which indicates that earning money is hard work? Remove any papers concerning a finance deal that you defaulted on or company stocks and shares that are doing badly, and any letters about overspending, loans, or a stack of unpaid bills, indicating that you will never get on top of your finances. Make sure there are no pictures here that are symbolically negative –

men climbing up a mountain, beggars in a foreign country, or old black-and-white engravings of slaves or servants. Be careful of the imagery that you project in this area. An empty bowl, unused wallet or purse, or a dying plant can indicate few or no resources.

Wealth is in the southeast
Your Wealth area links to green, the Wood element, and the trigram Sun.

Getting positive

To change the vibrations here, you need to create an area that inspires financial success and which nourishes the other people or things that are important to you. Money has a strong energy, and as soon as you start to attract it, more will follow.

To feed Wealth energy into this space, place in your Wealth area your bank statements (even your check book overnight), lottery tickets, a business card or a picture of you, and a bowl of coins. For the abundance aspect, add photographs of beloved friends or pets, and one or two treasured ornaments. A water feature, such as an ornamental fountain or an aquarium, will bring more energy into the southeast corner of your living area (but don't put a water feature in the bedroom, as it can be negative here).

Wealth loser
Clutter piles, pictures saying life is hard work, and empty containers give out bad energy in your Wealth and Prosperity space. Loans files, piles of bills, or money wallets containing nothing but receipts stop money and good things flowing in.

PURITY POINTS 23–26

♦ Display wooden boxes, photograph frames, or statues to enhance the Wood energy.
♦ Place a money (jade) plant here, in a terra-cotta pot, putting a gold coin in the earth to symbolize growth (if the plant doesn't thrive, ask yourself whether you really want to have more money).
♦ Blue glassware, dishes, or a lamp will encourage more wealth (Water feeds Wood).
♦ Savings books or premium bonds can be kept here to absorb the Wealth energy.

CLAPPING FOR CASH

After removing all your clutter, you need to make your Wealth area an inspiring, yang place. Lift any stagnancy that is left by clapping all around it – clap harder where the noise seems muffled. As the energy lifts, light some candles and, as you gaze into the flames, say, "I am attracting wealth and abundance into my world." Repeat this ceremony when your bank balance starts to drop.

Wealth winner

When this area is free of unwanted possessions, boost your finances or things you love using the energies of the southeast. Add in symbolic images of wealth, healthy plants, bank books or statements, or cherished pictures of family or pets to let more prosperity and abundance enter your life.

KEY TO WEALTH AREA

1 A money plant or other healthy, round-leaved plant can enhance your finances.

2 A running water feature energizes this space.

3 A bowl of coins or some notes symbolize wealth.

4 A loved family picture feeds into the good energies present here.

5 Bank statements can also benefit from the space's positive vibrations.

6 Blue ornaments link to Water, energizing the space's Wood element.

PURITY POINTS 27–32

THREE OF THE BEST	THREE OF THE WORST
♦ Symbolic signs and wealth objects	♦ A picture that emphasizes struggle
♦ A treasured ornament or a picture	♦ An empty wallet or coin purse
♦ A running water feature to encourage Wealth chi	♦ Letters about debts or loans, or loads of bills

Bringing In Helpful People

The Mentors and Networking area, which is associated with helpful people, is in the northwest of your home, or of each room. It is linked to the element of Metal, to feelings of security and feeling whole, and to the mellow season of fall. This area represents a figure of authority, a leader, or someone who guides you in the right direction. More commonly it is about the helpful people in your life who give visible or unseen support – that unique network of human beings who help you to cope more easily. It is about contacts or friends already

REAL-LIFE NETWORKING

One time, in a client's kitchen, I found a load of yellowing newspapers and a trashcan in the Mentors area. When asked, my client admitted having problems with her builders, and that many of her friends suddenly seemed reluctant to call. She cleared up the area and put an inviting pinboard there, with notes, contact cards, and friends' letters. She put her mail here as well, and her interaction with people improved.

Linking up

Networking is not just about making contacts – it is also about mentors, the people who help or inspire us at every stage of life. A mentor can be a spiritual leader, a teacher, or a charismatic boss.

made, and those to come in the future, who bring you a sense of fulfillment and success, but also, and more importantly, contentment.

ALL CLUTTERED UP

Think about the effects on you if this space is overflowing with unwanted items. How well have you fared lately? Have you repeatedly not had phone calls returned by people you are trying to contact? Has a close friend let you down on several occasions? Have you felt frustrated when trying to attract new clients at work, sensing an unseen barrier to your aims? If your Mentors area is giving off dull, musty energy, you will feel that you are becoming invisible to friends who can motivate you.

NETWORKING CHECKLIST

Ask yourself these questions about the helpful people in your life. If you answer "Yes" to any, look at your Mentors areas for unwanted items. Remove any that you find, purify the corner, and wait for that phone to start ringing.

♦ Is your boss, who was once so encouraging and attentive, now unsupportive?

♦ Does an appointment with a plumber or repair man keep on being changed?

♦ Has the number of your close friends diminished recently?

♦ Do you find colleagues at work unwilling to share useful information with you?

♦ Has a regular babysitter suddenly stopped wanting to help out?

♦ Has a friend or colleague who regularly counsels you suddenly become unavailable ?

ACTION PLAN

Look around your home and assess what you are keeping in your Mentors area(s). Then get rid of any clutter there. Give away heaps of old, dusty magazines and any material relating to  interests that you now no longer pursue. Throw away empty redundant boxes, and sort through all your photographs, keeping only those that make you feel good about yourself. Now assess what else you are hoarding. Study carefully any symbolism in this area: perhaps you have hung a depressing mask here, which may be subconsciously affecting your mood and therefore how you react to personal and professional contacts. Remove lists of people with whom you have lost touch, because these just represent the past and therefore stale energy. If your address book is damaged in any way, then discard it – it is not fostering good relations. Get rid of any argumentative correspondence with your friends, your employees, or your boss. Also, dispose of broken statues of mentors or spiritual leaders, such as Buddha, as these can negatively affect future partnerships that could nurture you.

Mentors are in the northwest
Your Mentors area links to white and metallic colors, the Metal element, and the trigram Chien.

Getting positive

Once you have removed all the negative material from this area, create a space that exudes good relations and networking. If you are working with a life coach at the moment, or even a personal trainer, put their brochure or details here. You can encourage good communication in this corner with your fax machine, computer, phone, diary, current address book, list of contacts, and a printed reminder of those new people whom you are trying to bring into your life right now.

If you feel that you need the guidance of a spiritual mentor, place a symbolic picture of an angel, the Dalai Lama, or someone who inspires you in a metal frame.

Your Mentors area is a good sector in which to keep cards of useful local contacts or tradespeople (weed out the ones who have let you down in the past). Keep the contacts up to date, throwing out old, unused cards.

Mentors loser
Piles of junk, contacts from your past, or details of people who have let you down create a dumping ground of negativity in your Mentors area. A cracked mirror, a sad mask, and an old phone also symbolically block any positive networking.

PURITY POINTS 33–36

♦ Add some silver or gold items to boost the Metal element – go for metal picture frames or a gold address book.
♦ Put a six-rod metal windchime here.
♦ Use ceramic ornaments or bowls to energize this corner (Earth feeds Metal in the productive cycle of elements).
♦ A laughing Buddha statue will enhance your mentor luck. These are available from Chinese stores – choose one in gold.

A WATER RITUAL FOR HELP

First, energize a bowl of water with a natural quartz crystal for 24 hours. Then take the bowl in your hands and, with a sprig of fresh or dried lavender, flick the water around your Mentors area to lift the energy after the junk has gone. Close your eyes and say to yourself for a few minutes, "I am letting new people and contacts enter my life." Revive the energy again if the phone calls slow down.

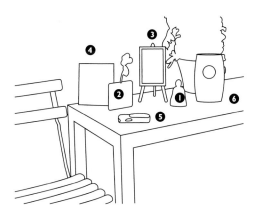

KEY TO HELPFUL PEOPLE AREA

1 A statue of a spiritual leader, such as Buddha or Jesus Christ, emphasizes the important mentor energy here.

2 A glass or ceramic ornament, such as this modern glass vase, brings in boosting Earth energy. (Earth produces Metal in the productive cycle of elements.)

3 A picture of a boss or leader, such as the Dalai Lama, in a metal frame can inspire you, and supports the Metal energy here.

4 Calendars or diaries placed here can receive the good networking vibrations.

5 Placing your home phone or cell phone here overnight encourages people to contact you.

6 Other favorite metal ornaments, such as a metal vase, can be placed here to keep the Mentor energy flowing.

Mentors winner

With a clear space, bring in helpful people by using the positive northwest energies. Put in mentor images, a current address book or personal organizer, phones, and contact disk or lists to allow in inspiring contacts.

PURITY POINTS 37–42

THREE OF THE BEST	THREE OF THE WORST
♦ Ceramic mentor statue	♦ Files concerning a bad client
♦ Diaries, address books, calendars, or personal organizers	♦ Torn address book
♦ A telephone or cell phone	♦ List of old contacts whom you are no longer in touch with

Firing Up Your Career

The area relating to work success is in the north of your home, or of each room. It is linked to the Water element, to the cold of winter, the ebb and flow of life, our chosen journey. This is your Career Prospects area, where your ambitions and dreams begin. It is the place of achievement, where hard work in your job or profession is recognized, where your willpower and drive enable you to attain what you really desire. The way water moves is connected with the flow of chi – it is an activator that encourages prosperity. So when life is going well, we are "going with the flow." This area is also involved with life's bigger picture – the reason why we are here, and what we really want – our voyage of discovery.

REAL-LIFE SUCCESS
A friend of mine was rather stuck in her career. Feeling frustrated, she decided one day to clear several areas in her apartment of junk – particularly her Career Prospects area. Afterward she felt liberated, the energy shifted, and a couple of weeks later she was delighted to hear that she was being promoted to editorial director of the publishing company for which she worked.

Boosting your career
The energy in your Career area can affect your progress. De-junking and purifying this space banishes any stagnant energy hampering success.

ALL CLUTTERED UP
As your home can contribute to the way you progress in your career, it is important to find out what you are storing in this area, because any piles of clutter will slow down your success at work. Take a short time to review how your job has been going lately. Have you been reluctant to go to work each day? Do you find that you are constantly clashing with work colleagues? Does your boss seem to block any new idea or project that you suggest? If your Career space is lacking positive energy, you will feel at a low ebb and won't have your usual business acumen or incisive manner in dealing with your clients.

CAREER CHECKLIST

Ask yourself the following questions about the state of your working life. If you answer "Yes" to any, examine your Career Prospects areas for junk. If you find any clutter, get rid of it, cleanse the space, and see what happens with your job.

♦ Have you recently been turned down for promotion at work?

♦ Are you finding your normal workload harder than usual to get through?

♦ Do you find that colleagues ignore your valid points in meetings?

♦ Is your boss being unsupportive?

♦ Have you been for several job interviews and not been offered one position?

♦ Are you constantly working late, but without ever being thanked?

ACTION PLAN

Appraise your Career Prospects area(s) and see what junk is gathering there. Have a general clearout in all your rooms, and make a priority of your office if you work from home, because any clutter here could be disastrous to your business success. If you work in an office, do the same there. First, scan the room and see what is on the floor: are there any discarded boxes, old files, out-of-date brochures or periodicals, old stationery, or piles of unfiled correspondence? Throw away what's not needed and file the rest.

On closer inspection, try to establish if you are giving out a subliminal message that you can't achieve success. Take an old computer or disused disks to the dump, remove any letters regarding layoffs, and anything that connects you to a job in the past. This might be forgotten work files, pictures of former colleagues, old company brochures, or even a file of poor appraisals projecting an image of you not doing well. Dispense with any books on an old career or interest, because you need to go forward, not backward. Make sure there isn't an overflowing trashcan here, for this will give out the message that your job will never come to anything, or that you will not get what you want.

Career is in the north
Your Career area links to blue, the Water element, and the trigram K'an.

Getting positive

Your aim is to build a positive space that projects the image that you are good at what you do and says to the world, "I have a successful career and a life that I thoroughly enjoy." You can say this regularly to yourself as an affirmation to build up your self-esteem.

To attract the right emanations, put a current resumé and any congratulatory memos or emails from your boss in your Career Prospects area. For extra supportive energy, place your business cards in a metal box. If you want to change your profession, add desirable job advertisements or a picture representing your chosen career. You can also leave your workbag, career textbooks, laptop computer, and personal organizer here to gain beneficial energy overnight.

PURITY POINTS 43–46

♦ Hang up a metal windchime with hollow tubes to energize the area (Metal feeds Water).
♦ Create some yang energy with an aquarium, ideally containing eight goldfish and one black fish.
♦ Display some blue or black ornaments or accessories to strengthen the Water energy that exists here.
♦ Add a strong-looking male or female statue or small figurine (depending on your sex). This helps you show to the world a positive image of yourself.

Career loser
Rubbish all over the place, dead work files, and old company newsletters give out stagnant energy in your career space. A damaged old computer and disks, a bad appraisal file or layoff correspondence says your career is going nowhere.

CLEANSING FOR A GREAT CAREER

When the clutter has gone from your Career Prospects area, make this corner really stand out with a simple cleansing ceremony. Light a sage smudge stick, briefly smudge around your body to purify your aura, then blow the smoke all around the area, saying out loud as you watch it, "I am going to be outstanding in my career." Put the stick in a holder for a few minutes, watching the uplifting smoke. Repeat if your career light starts to fade.

KEY TO CAREER AREA

1 A laptop computer positioned here can receive good career energy.

2 A water feature strengthens the corner's existing element.

3 A desired job can come closer if you place the advert here.

4 Business cards promote your career status.

5 A professional picture of you emphasizes your career skills.

6 A cell phone left here overnight symbolizes a business person who keeps in contact, and who is in control.

Career winner

In your newly cleared area, support your career with the healthy vibrations of this north corner. Add in your computer, positive professional images of yourself, well-designed business stationery, desired job adverts, or current work brochures to shout out your business success.

PURITY POINTS 47–52

THREE OF THE BEST	THREE OF THE WORST
◆ Your current computer	◆ Pictures of old work colleagues
◆ Business cards, workbag	◆ Broken computer, damaged disks
◆ Professional picture of yourself	◆ Bad appraisal letter, old client files

Boosting the Learning Zone

Your Education and Knowledge area is in the northeast of your home, or of each room. It relates to the Earth element, to wisdom and thoughtfulness, warm late-summer afternoons, and the maturing process of all plants. This is the seat of education, the place where teaching and learning begin in childhood, and where knowledge on all subjects is sought and gathered throughout your own and your children's lives. On a deeper level, it is about self-development as you grow and change emotionally and mentally. It concerns the way you explore your inner depths to free any emotional blockages that are stopping you making the progression forward that you now need.

REAL-LIFE LEARNING

A friend was replanning her life and had decided to leave her corporate job, but couldn't seem to commit herself to the new training class in which she was interested. When she looked at her Knowledge area, she had piles of old brochures on classes she had never attended. She removed these, felt an energy shift, and soon felt able to book herself onto her life-changing class.

Getting new knowledge

Clearing and purifying the area of your home that corresponds to your learning zone will help you to study well and succeed in examinations.

ALL CLUTTERED UP

Learning should be enjoyable and help to expand your mind, but it can be hard work if you let this area accumulate junk that is no longer necessary in your life. Think about any classes you have attended recently. Have they been a pleasure or a real struggle for you? If you have children, are you getting reports that they seem to have difficulty concentrating on their studies? Are you trying self-development exercises, but finding that your heart isn't really in them? If your Knowledge area is not feeding you beneficial energy, then you will seek out any distraction in order to avoid learning or signing up for a class. Children who normally love going to school may suddenly develop a reluctance as the stagnation in this area starts to affect them.

KNOWLEDGE CHECKLIST

Ask yourself the following questions about your own and your children's attitude to learning at the moment. If you answer "Yes" to any, assess your Knowledge areas for clutter. Remove any unwanted articles, cleanse the space, and see how quickly your zest for new interests returns.

♦ Has your children's success at school diminished over the last few months?

♦ Do you normally love taking new classes, but seem to have lost interest in starting anything new?

♦ Has a teenager been accepted at several universities, but refused to go?

♦ Have you been asked to train people at work, but don't really have the enthusiasm to do it?

♦ Do you enjoy reading to improve your mind, but have hardly picked up a book recently?

♦ Are you normally a firm believer in meditation, visualization, or other self-help techniques, but just have not made time to do them lately?

ACTION PLAN

Check your Knowledge area(s) to see what is stored there. Then throw or give away any ornaments or other paraphernalia that you never liked, even if they came from someone close to you. Throw out old periodicals, particularly any linked to a past hobby or interest. And dispose of any dying flowers, or fruit that is rotting. Analyze what else you have here: are you subconsciously holding back your quest for new knowledge? If you still have school textbooks stored here, give them away because they are connected to the past – to a younger you. If you love holding on to things from your college days, search for any rejection notices, torn degrees, or damaged achievement awards that may be inhibiting your current thirst for enlightenment. Remove details of any classes you didn't

complete, for they will prevent you from starting new ones. If you are clearing an area that is used by children, get rid of any broken or wornout pens or crayons, damaged rulers, other bits of stationery, and any workbooks they no longer use.

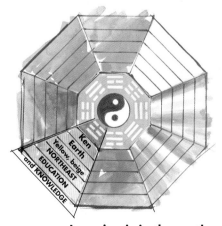

Learning is in the northeast
Your Education and Knowledge area links to yellow and beige, the Earth element, and the trigram Ken.

Getting positive

You need to make a space that leaves behind past learning and exudes good vibrations for the knowledge to come. If you are thinking about taking any new classes, such as art, yoga, or massage at a local college, then place their brochure in your Knowledge area in order to ensure its success. The outline of a new work or computer course will also benefit from this energy.

Details of any classes that your children want to attend, such as Spanish language classes, gymnastics, piano or dancing lessons, can also be placed here. Bring any self-development books that really inspire you, and which are turning you into the person you want to be, into this space.

Education loser
An overloaded corner, old school text books, and broken study materials turn down your learning vibrations in your Education and Knowledge space. Torn diplomas, discarded degrees, rejection letters, and old study files indicate your learning has reached a dead end.

PURITY POINTS 53–57

♦ Put a natural quartz crystal here to accelerate the good energy for your own or your children's learning.
♦ Display on the wall any diplomas you have recently received, and light them well with spotlights.
♦ Put a round red lamp or some candles in red ceramic holders in this corner (Fire feeds Earth).
♦ Yellow ceramic or terra-cotta ornaments will strengthen the Earth energy.
♦ Position your home desk in the northeast, the learning corner, of your study.

SALT FOR MAGNETIZING KNOWLEDGE

With all the refuse cleared out, cleanse the ambience of your Knowledge area by sprinkling some rock salt around the perimeter, starting from the left and leaving a pile in the middle. As you sprinkle the salt, think about what you want to attract to this space, and then say, "I am acquiring all the knowledge I now need." Hold onto the thought for a few minutes. Remove the salt after 24 hours, but repeat the process if you need a surge in learning energy.

KEY TO EDUCATION AREA

1 A study instrument placed here absorbs the beneficial Earth energies of the space.

2 Current text books or self-development books in this corner increase your studying aptitude.

3 A red lamp positioned here brings in boosting Fire element energy.

4 Language or learning discs and a CD player in this area strengthen your learning abilities.

5 Candles bring in stimulating Fire energy.

6 Materials, such as for an art class, kept here increase creative inspiration.

7 A natural quartz crystal enhances the existing Earth energies.

PURITY POINTS 58–63

THREE OF THE BEST	THREE OF THE WORST
♦ Current study books or brochures ♦ Study materials or instruments ♦ Self-development books	♦ Old study files ♦ Ancient school text books ♦ Torn, discarded diplomas or degrees

Education winner

When you have removed stagnancy from this space, accelerate your learning using the positive energies of this northeast corner. Feature current study or workshop materials, learning aids, or new class brochures to create a positive ambience for acquiring new knowledge.

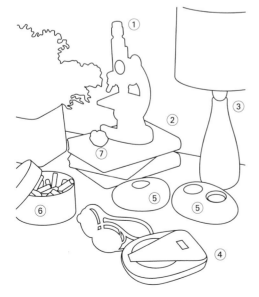

Encouraging New Beginnings

The area linked to Children and New Beginnings is in the west of your home, or of each room. It is associated with the Metal element, with happiness, hope, joy, and with glorious fall sunsets. This is the place of female energies, representing the children you want to have or nurturing the ones already born. It is about the longing to give birth, fertility, and bringing something new and precious into the world. But the Children area isn't always about offspring in the physical sense; it is also about imagination and having the ability to create something of your own. Here you can plant embryonic ideas for a business, a passion, or an interest, and watch how – with careful nurturing – they slowly develop and come to fruition.

REAL-LIFE CREATIVITY

A client was in a rush to sell her house because she was moving abroad. Not many people were coming to view it, so I told her to put the selling details of the house in her Children area. Soon the positive energy started to work and she was inundated with potential buyers.

Seeds for the future
New beginnings include new projects and fertility or children. Boosting this area of your home will bring you new opportunities.

ALL CLUTTERED UP

Your creativity and fertility can be completely blocked if you have let this space get crowded with items you no longer want or use. How has this area of your life felt recently? Are you trying to start a new project, such as writing a book, but just can't seem to pen that first line? If you are a mother, have your children been moody, but don't seem to want to discuss their problems with you? Or, if you are in a partnership and want children, do you keep postponing the moment to talk about starting a family? If the energy level has dropped in this

CHILDREN AND CREATIVITY CHECKLIST

Ask yourself the following questions about the actions of your children (if you have any), or about your fertility and creative life. If you answer "Yes" to any, search through your Children areas for clutter. Get rid of any that you find, do a simple purification ceremony, and see how quickly harmony and balance are restored.

♦ Have you felt that your creativity has been stifled lately?

♦ Are you trying to get pregnant, but having little success?

♦ Do your children seem to argue all the time, and constantly answer you back?

♦ Are your children not doing well academically at school?

♦ Do you feel that you are lacking in ideas for new projects?

♦ Does it feel as if there is a blockage in your mind, which is not allowing inspiration to pass through?

creative space, you will not feel able to take that first step forward to bring in the family or new ventures that you desire.

ACTION PLAN

Appraise your Children area(s) closely and see what objects you have been storing there. Remove anything you don't need or want. Discard junk mail, cards from friends that no longer have any meaning, old CDs and cassettes – break that tie with your past life. Check if there are any items that are stopping you being creative or upsetting your children. A full trashcan will make your brain stagnate. Search for any failed projects, such as a rejected script, manuscript, or business plan. Dispose of any bad school reports or teachers' letters undermining your children's performance at school. If you are longing for a baby, make

sure that the under-bed area is not your bedroom's dumping ground. Negative, sluggish energy seeping up through the bed will not create the right environment in which to conceive. Remove any broken toys or sad paintings from your children's bedrooms.

Children and New Beginnings are in the west
Your Children and New Beginnings area links to white, Metal, and the trigram Tui.

Getting positive

As soon as you have discarded unwanted material you will start to feel the energy and atmosphere changing here. To foster more positivity for your projects, place in your Children and New Beginnings area details of any properties that you want to buy, of forthcoming exhibitions, new proposals, or book or play ideas. To encourage fertility, add a picture of you and your partner, and tuck a symbolic baby photograph behind it; alternatively, you can add a pair of Tibetan booties, some new baby books, replica Fabergé eggs, or a set of Russian nesting dolls. If you are already expecting a baby, add your ultrasound images. If you already have some children, put a happy photograph of them in a metal frame. Include a fish, a teddy bear, or other crystal ornament linked to the Earth element to increase the strong vibrations here.

Children and New Beginnings loser
Old junk, ancient projects, and negative children's pictures release bad energy. An old house plaque, broken ornaments or toys restrict fertile beginnings.

PURITY POINTS 64–68

♦ Place a picture of (or some real) sprouting bulbs, such as daffodils or hyacinth, here to cultivate new beginnings.
♦ Display some ceramic and terra-cotta ornaments to augment the Metal energy (Earth feeds Metal).
♦ Place a natural quartz or amethyst crystal in this area to help motivate your children at school.
♦ Use white, silver, or gold objects or fabrics to enhance the west corner of your living room.
♦ Leave some little brass bells in this area, and ring them when you feel that the space needs a lift.

A RITUAL FOR INSPIRATION

Once the clutter has been removed, clear the atmosphere completely in your creative space by using a singing bowl. Take a mallet and tap it around the edge of the bowl, slowly building up a strong humming sound. As the noise intensifies, close your eyes and say to yourself, "I am an inspired and fertile person." Use the humming tone again when you have creativity burnout.

PURITY POINTS 69–74

THREE OF THE BEST
♦ Happy children photos or items to encourage fertility
♦ New project files
♦ Aspirational images

THREE OF THE WORST
♦ Bad school reports
♦ Piles of discarded projects files
♦ Unhappy drawings by children

Children and New Beginnings winner
With no junk, foster fertility or new schemes by tapping into these energies of the west. Place happy children pictures, sprouting plants, new projects or dream brochures to pull in your desires.

KEY TO CHILDREN AND NEW BEGINNINGS
1 Flowering plants placed here signify fertility and new beginnings.

2 Happy photos of existing children encourage a good future.

3 Photos, images, or brochures of a dream home or another project in this space will help to bring it in.

4 A glass ornament feeds in boosting Earth energies.

5 A crystal helps enhance the Earth vibrations here.

6 An ideas book soaks up good project vibrations.

Creating Family Bliss

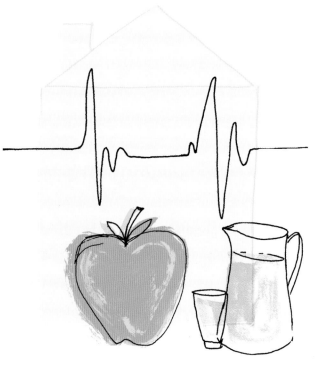

The east of your home, or of each room, is the space of Family and Health. It connects to the Wood element, to patience and courage, energy at the start of a new day, sunrise, and the blossoming of plants in springtime. This is where you aim to achieve close relationships with your partner and children, and where respect is cultivated for parents, grandparents, and other relatives. The Family and Health area is also about the importance of good health, of controlling daily stress, keeping illness at bay, and achieving balance, wellbeing, and body harmony.

REAL-LIFE FAMILY HAPPINESS

For months a friend seemed to suffer from every possible family problem, and just when she got over one situation something else happened. When I was at her home one evening, I discovered that the Family area in their youngest child's room was used for changing diapers. Even though these were disposed of and not left here, they were dissipating that corner's vibrancy. Once she moved the changing area to a neutral space in the middle of the room, family relations became much better.

Getting good health

Removing junk from your Family and Health area unblocks negative energy that can cause ill health or family problems.

ALL CLUTTERED UP

Family life should flow freely and be enjoyable, with only the occasional upset or altercation. But you can disturb the equilibrium of this important corner by using it as your dumping ground for junk. Try and recall how family life has seemed recently. Has it been very disruptive, with constant arguments and misunderstandings? Are you finding that your children won't respond to discipline and are constantly acting up? And consider the health of your family: has there seemed to be hardly a break from illness, with a younger child

FAMILY AND HEALTH CHECKLIST

Ask yourself the following questions about the state of your family life and how healthy you have been lately. If you answer "Yes" to any, check your family areas and dispose of any debilitating clutter, then perform a short purification ritual, and see how quickly your family becomes loving and close once more.

♦ Do you normally try every new type of workout, but just haven't had the energy in the last few months?

♦ Are your children missing sports' classes that they normally love?

♦ Have family mealtimes started to fall apart, with everyone avoiding each other and eating at different times?

♦ Has a close relative been to stay and been disagreeable all the time?

♦ Are the family trying to get out of special weekend trips together that you all used to love?

♦ Do friends no longer stay very long at your home, because they pick up on the tense family atmosphere?

recovering from flu, for example, just before the eldest comes down with it? Slow, dull vibrations coming from the Family area will cause dissatisfaction and upset for seemingly no reason, and will adversely affect how your whole family approaches life. They will also make you feel down, which can deplete your immune system.

ACTION PLAN

Look at your Family area(s) and see whether it holds excess clutter. Dispense with any dead plants or half-finished home-repair projects, and give away games or puzzle books that are never used. Now see if there is anything here that is having a bad influence on your family. Make sure this is not the place where you hoard old pill bottles, doctors' correspondence, notes, and X-rays from your physician that may

be subliminally promoting ill health. If you love murder novels, remove them (and any books about family problems) from this space as they are just too negative here. Seek out torn or sad family photographs, damaged albums, or broken family statues, because these can dampen everyone's morale.

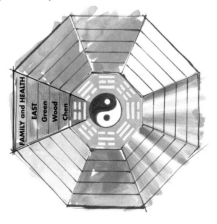

Family and Health is in the east
Your Family and Health area links to green, the Wood element, and the trigram Chen.

Getting positive

After your clearout, you need to take action to make this area work for you and your family. Placing happy family photographs in wooden frames, or on a wooden-framed pinboard, will ensure loving feelings and better communication. Strengthen family ties with a tapestry of the family tree, details of your ancestors' history, or genealogy books. To promote exercise and good health, position here any leaflets or brochures for gyms, health resorts, and workouts, plus relaxation tapes. Symbols of a healthy mind and body (wooden massage footrollers, or a yoga video) can also sit in this space.

Family and Health loser

Loads of junk, dying plants, and medication that is out of date send out decaying vibrations from your Family and Health space. Horror novels and torn or creased family photos do not foster the family love and good health that should exist here.

PURITY POINTS 75–78

♦ Put a healthy round-leaved plant here to strengthen the Wood energy, and display wooden boxes or bowls.

♦ Add a water fountain to encourage better family interaction (Water feeds Wood).

♦ Position your bed in the east (a good space, after your Marriage and Romantic Happiness area).

♦ Place an amethyst crystal in this area, for healing and to absorb any negativity; or a tiger's eye, to balance yin and yang energy.

CHANTING FOR HEALTH

Discard all the clutter and then purify your Family area by chanting. Use a word such as the meditation mantra "Om". Close your eyes and say it, letting the sound build as you move clockwise around the area. Say to yourself, as the energy lightens, "My family is healthy and full of love." Keep thinking this as you repeat the chant for several more minutes. Chant again if you feel your special family vibrations starting to drop.

Family and Health winner

When the junk has been removed, encourage good family emanations in this east corner. Put in happy family pictures, bowls of fruit, and exercise items to promote a healthy family environment.

KEY TO FAMILY AND HEALTH

1 A healthy flowering plant supports Wood energy.

2 A happy family picture in a wooden frame taps into the positive vibrations here.

3 Vitamins and mineral supplements placed here assure continuing good health.

4 Massage or exercise articles in this space promote the wellbeing of the family.

5 Fresh fruit in this corner symbolizes good health and enjoyment of food.

6 A blue ornament or water fountain brings in some boosting Water energy here.

PURITY POINTS 79–84

THREE OF THE BEST

♦ A happy, recent family photograph
♦ Exercise items, health books, relaxation tapes
♦ Blue ornaments or accessories

THREE OF THE WORST

♦ Old pill bottles and medicines
♦ Unhappy family photographs or battered album
♦ Broken family ornaments or statues

Clearing Out

Now that you have worked out your aims (see pages 10–11) and assessed what you have been keeping in all your key aspirational areas (see pages 16–47), it is time to start the process of removing the unwanted baggage from your life. Remember that this can be an emotional experience; you must be willing to change and to let your clutter go.

Look at your goals and work through your most immediate ones. Then move on to your short-term goals, noting the schedule that you have allowed yourself. They should include some of your worst areas for clutter, because the sooner you get one area cleared, the better you will feel. If one of your long-term clutter tips is the hall, the benefits of clearing that space will be immediate, as the energy will start to flow more freely again. You will sense a fog lifting, and optimism and vitality about your future will return.

MOVING ON

Belongings are often harder to remove from our lives when they have a long-term sentimental

Bag it up and let it go
Take your time when clearing your clutter and allocating possessions to five bags. Work on a little at a time – don't let the bags stagnate and become another form of clutter. Releasing your clutter is often an emotional experience as you let go of memories as well as the actual belongings.

attachment – when they are connected to our past or with a loving relationship. Letting them go will be emotional and you may find that you have intense feelings about certain items, perhaps more so than you had expected. But releasing possessions lets you live in the "now," and the bonus is that there will be a wonderful feeling of renewal and regeneration.

SENTIMENTAL POSSESSIONS	RELEASING TECHNIQUES
♦ Love letters from past relationships	Read through one last time, if you can bear it, then either throw them all out or (if this is impossible) keep a few in a mementoes box.
♦ Birthday, Christmas, and other special cards	We often hold on to these types of cards because of the caring messages that they contain. Keep a few really special ones and let go of the rest.
♦ Photographs	Only keep ones of happy times, and throw away pictures of people you can't remember, out-of-focus shots, or repeat images of a certain place.
♦ Disliked ornament from a relative	It's hard, but you need to give it to someone who will get pleasure from it, otherwise every time you look at it you will just receive negative feelings.
♦ Present from a past boyfriend, girlfriend, husband, or wife	If you get a warm feeling every time you look at this statue, picture, or piece of jewelry, then that's fine – keep it. But if you only get angry remembering how they left you or hurt you, then give it away and liberate yourself from these negative feelings.
♦ School memorabilia	It's fine to show your children your school prizes, textbooks, awards, badges, or diplomas. Then get rid of them, except for a couple. You still have the memories – you don't need the tangible items.
♦ Children's toys, drawings, and letters	Keep a couple of letters and drawings, and throw out the rest. Give any toys that are in good condition to a hospital, library, nursery, or crèche.

The five-bag system

To prepare yourself for your clutter-clearing, make sure you have enough heavy-duty trash bags, or strong cardboard boxes, to sort your junk into appropriate piles. Leave anything you want to keep (and not move) where it is.

PURITY POINTS 85–87

♦ Fit your clothes to the closet space available. If the doors still bulge, more clothes need to be discarded.
♦ Throw out any unopened boxes from your last house move.
♦ Think about taking any useful objects to a local sale and making some money from them, and take plastics, paper, glass, and cans to a recycling center.

Now label your bags:

♦ **1st bag** "Junk" – all the useless items that can go to the refuse dump.
♦ **2nd bag** "Thrift (charity) shop or friends" – useful belongings that you no longer want, but which other people might use.
♦ **3rd bag** "Things to be repaired or altered" – includes items, such as furniture, for renovating.
♦ **4th bag** "Things to sort and move" – these are useful articles that need to go some place else.

Bag 1: Junk

♦ **5th bag** "Transitional items" – belongings that you can't quite let go of; put this bag away for six months and, if you miss them, get them out again; otherwise give them away.

Bag 2: Friends

Bag 3: Items for repair

WHAT IS JUNK?

Before your clearout, focus on what is categorized as junk. It fits this description if:

♦ It is broken beyond repair
♦ You get negative feelings every time you look at it
♦ It is past its sell-by date
♦ It is an unwanted present
♦ It is out of date or doesn't fit.

Office junk is:

♦ Objects that are no longer used
♦ Items from old or abandoned projects
♦ Out-of-date reference materials
♦ Unwanted correspondence or old stationery
♦ Outmoded software and old emails.

It is not junk if:

♦ You love it every time you see it
♦ It is something you enjoy using
♦ It adds to your appreciation of daily life
♦ It helps your work or makes it easier.

LETTING GO

Work through one room, or closet, at a time, and start by dealing with the worst piles of clutter first. Try emptying boxes onto a drop cloth in the back yard, or in a large spare room, to see what you have kept in there. Don't spend hours reading old periodicals, letters, cards, or looking at drawings or other mementoes that once meant something or you will never throw them out. Throw away any unopened boxes, think about selling any useful items, and take any plastics, paper, glass, and cans to a recycling center.

Bag 4: Items to sort and move

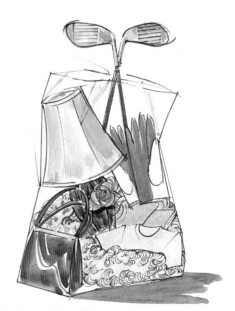

Bag 5: Transitional items

The Power of Cleansing

Once you have cleared out all the excess junk from your home, the difference in the way it looks and in the way you feel will be incredible, although it can be a daunting and emotional process if the clutter has accumulated over the years. Suddenly it will seem as though a weight has lifted from you – any confusion about which direction you should take will disappear, and all the new possibilities for your life will start to flood in. But before you think you can sit back and rest, there is something else you need to do to enhance the atmosphere that surrounds you.

KICKSTARTING THE ENERGY

Even when your clutter has gone, a slow, musty residual energy can linger, especially when the junk has been festering there for a long time. If this staleness is not removed, it will pull you down and sap your vitality. So to make your home a fresh, appealing environment once again, its overall energy needs a kickstart and will benefit from a deep cleansing ceremony.

CHOOSING A CEREMONY

There are several different types of ceremony that you can perform – it is up to you which one you choose. Each type works well, but some purify more deeply than others, so gauge the depth of cleansing that you need.

♦ **Smudging** is a powerful Native American method, where the smoke from a burning herb stick is wafted around the room to remove stagnancy and negativity.

♦ **Salt** sprinkled in piles in corners, or around the room, is another traditional purifier.

♦ **Incense and candles** are better as daily cleansers, but may also be used to enhance other purification methods.

♦ **Aromatherapy** uses plants' essential oils, which are versatile purifiers that leave behind a wonderful fragrance.

♦ **Sound** is another potent way of lifting dull energy. Choose a technique that really appeals to you: some rituals are very simple, while others require a musical instrument such as a bell or drum. Clapping around a room, for example, is a simple way of removing stagnancy; the clear tone of a ringing bell is used in many parts of the Eastern world to keep energy vibrant; the wonderful humming tone of a metal singing bowl is famous in countries such as Tibet for creating a strong vibration; and the deep, rhythmic sound of a drum is perfect for creating a higher energy level in a room. But you don't have to use an instrument –

a ceremony that involves chanting, intoning, or singing can be just as effective, and will pleasantly rejuvenate or revitalize the ambience of your home.

♦ **Water** is the final purifying tool that can help to remove negative vibrations. Simply misting a room using dilute aromatherapy oils acts as an immediate energizer, while performing a ceremony with water charged by the sun or by a quartz crystal is even more potent for cleansing the atmosphere.

Powerful aromas

Incense burning is one of the most popular and simple purification techniques used in temples throughout Asia, and also in many Catholic churches where the strong scent of Frankincense pervades morning and evening Mass.

Times to purify

There are various occasions when it can seem right to purify. Some people will instantly feel a drop in energy levels, while others will not be so sensitive. Obviously you may need an instant energy boost after an argument or an emotional upset, or when you have heard some sad news. Burning your favorite incense will blow away any of the negative emanations left behind, or as an alternative you could light several lavender-scented candles.

ILLNESS IN THE HOME

When someone has been ill in your home, a heavy, dull atmosphere remains. The energy becomes very yin and passive, and will start to affect your mood, so performing a cleansing ceremony is essential to make the air healthier. Smudging with sweetgrass will shift the heaviness, or you could try misting with stimulating, tangy essential oils such as lime, lemon, or orange.

REMOVING BLOCKAGES

There are occasions when we are stuck in our lives and unable to move on to new projects or interests. To overcome this, allow more time for activities that inspire you, and use yoga or meditation for spiritual development. To boost your home's positive energy, try using a singing bowl (see pages 76–79) and walk around each

Japanese stick incense
Japanese incense is delicately scented, and the wands tend to be fragile. It is easier to burn this variety in a heatproof bowl filled with colored sand.

room, sensing how the clear humming sound instantly changes the atmosphere for the better.

WHEN ON THE MOVE

You can use purifying or space-clearing techniques to transform hotel rooms that you are staying in while traveling. Clear out the stale

Types of incense

Incense comes in coils (right), that are burned on a saucer or custom-made coil burner; sticks of varying thicknesses (right); Tibetan incense is usually broader than other varieties; and short Indian incense sticks (far right), know as dhoop sticks.

energy of the previous occupants by misting the room with sage essential oil. Then light a small lavender-scented candle to balance the existing energies of the room.

MOVING HOUSE

A purifying ceremony can help a move two ways: if you are trying to sell your house, and if you have just moved into a new one. If you have lived happily and healthily in your home, then you will not have to do much to encourage someone else to like its energy and buy it.

Clean the house thoroughly, because dust lowers the vibrancy of the atmosphere, then go around each room clapping up the energy. Spend more time clapping in each corner, or wherever it sounds muffled.

Moving into a new home requires a stronger cleansing process because it is difficult to know the history of the house. There may be some sad or negative energy lingering in the walls that needs to be dispersed, because it will affect both you and your family in time. Smudging is the most powerful purifier, so use a sage or rosemary smudge stick, wave the smoke into every nook and cranny, and wish yourself good health and happiness in your new home.

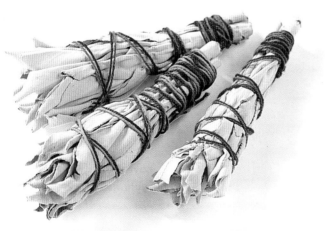

Sage smudge sticks

Sage-only smudge sticks are traditional purifiers and are made in the same way as those comprising traditional sweetgrass and other varieties of herbs.

Preparing for Purification

Performing a purification ceremony in your home is a special, happy occasion, so choose the day carefully. It needs to be done during daylight hours, so if you have a boisterous family you may want to send them out for the day so that you do not have any distractions, or choose a time when you know that the rest of the family will be out. Make sure you feel emotionally, mentally, and physically strong as it can sometimes be a bit tiring. Even if you are only suffering from a minor ailment, such as a cold or the early stages of flu, it is better to postpone it.

GATHERING INGREDIENTS AND INSTRUMENTS

Once you have decided on the type of ceremony you want to use, allow yourself some time to get together what you need. Incense, candles, salt, and essential oils are readily available but smudge sticks can be harder to find, so check for local suppliers, or if you have a good herb garden make some of your own (see page 58–59). Using a sound instrument, such as a drum, is a bigger investment but it is such a potent energizer that you will want to use it regularly. It is also worth enquiring if you can hire an instrument just for the day that you have chosen.

PURITY POINTS 88–92

Before you start your ceremony, make sure you are well prepared. It is important to cleanse your body and aura before you embark on cleansing the space around you. This prevents any old emotional or physical energy lingering as you work, which may make your purification practice less effective.

Only attempt purification when you feel emotionally and physically healthy. It is best not to purify your home when you are menstruating, if you have an open wound or during pregnancy, because your body is not at its optimum for this highly charged ceremony.

♦ Start with a clean space, so first open all the windows to let the air help with the ceremony, and dust, sweep, and vacuum each room.

♦ Remove any dead plants, and place some inspiring fresh flowers around.

♦ Remove any jewelry, take a bath or shower to cleanse and refresh your body, and ideally work barefoot to help you feel the energy.

♦ Turn off any music, unplug the telephone, and turn off your cell phone during your ceremony.

♦ Cleanse your aura of any negativity with a smouldering smudge stick or incense, or by aromatherapy misting around your head and body. Start on your left side, moving to the right, then around and behind your head.

SENSING ENERGY

Our hands are very sensitive and give off their own electromagnetic energy, so before your ceremony, connect with each room by going round with your hands extended (so your fingers are facing upward). Where there is stagnant or negative energy, your hands may feel heavier or a bit uncomfortable. Also, try sensing the energy coming off corners – move the palms of your hands toward the corner and see when you feel the energy; you normally sense a cold draught just a short distance away from the corner.

SETTING YOUR INTENTION

This is the most important part of your purifying day. Really focus on what you want to achieve from this cleansing. You should feel really proud of yourself; you have cleared out all your clutter, you know your life is about to change for the better, so what else do you want to bring in?

If you find it easier, you can write down your intent and read it out as you do your ceremony. Remember, this is a special day for you and your home, so embrace it and enjoy it to the full. You are going to be a new, more vibrant person at the end of it.

Pure space

When you set your intention, find a quiet space in which to consider your wishes for the future. Give yourself time to really reflect on new opportunities, the people you want to attract, and why.

The Art of Smudging

This is a very potent ancient Native American tradition where smoke is used to cleanse a space of any negative energies lingering there. Smudge sticks made from special dried herbs are burnt to produce smoke that purifies the atmosphere of a room. The smoke can also cleanse your aura (your subtle energy field) of any distressing emotions before you start smudging. The herbs sage and sweetgrass were often featured in old tribal ceremonies, and are still popular ones to use today. Sage is one of the strongest cleansing herbs, it is linked to purity and spirit, while sweetgrass is believed to get rid of negativity and banish bad spirits. It is a popular herb for purification in shamanic sweatlodge ceremonies. Mugwort and rosemary, which are often found growing in the garden, are other herbs that are powerful cleansers.

To perform a home purification ceremony, the smudge stick is lit to release its healing smoke into all corners of each room.

PURITY POINT 93

♦ Rather than use your free hand to waft the smudging smoke around a room, you can do this using a large single feather to circulate the smoke.

BUYING SMUDGE STICKS

You can buy smudge sticks from alternative stores or by mail order, but once you are a regular "smudger", it can be very special and more personal to make your own (see box). Pick the herbs that feel right for what you want to do. Drying

Sweetgrass coil

them, and then making them into your own smudge sticks can help to connect you to the spirit of the plants, making the purification ceremony you need to do a much more intimate and fulfilling occasion.

Smudge stick

MAKING YOUR OWN SMUDGE STICKS

You may find it easier to make small smudge sticks that you just use a few times, as the bigger ones which are lit repeatedly can start to lose their positive vibrations. The herbs used opposite are good purifiers, but if there are good indigenous herbs growing in your area, include these in your selection, and always honor the herb you are cutting, only taking a few sprigs at a time.

TO MAKE 6 SMALL STICKS

Ingredients
6 x 6 in (15 cm) sprigs of lavender
6 x 6 in (15 cm) sprigs of mugwort
12 x 6 in (15 cm) sprigs of sage
6 x 6 in (15 cm) sprigs of rosemary
Cord for binding

1 Tie the springs of lavender, mugwort, sage, and rosemary with cord and then hang upside down on hooks in bunches to dry for a few days or up to a week in a warm dry place. When they feel dry and brittle they are ready.

2 Take down the sprigs and place on a table. Sort out the herb sprigs into sticks, using 1 lavender, 1 mugwort, 2 sage, and 1 rosemary for each one.

3 Cut lengths of cord for each stick. Hold each stick in your hand and wrap the cord round firmly, starting by knotting the cord around the base. Wrap the cord from the base to the tip, then cross the cord at the top as shown and criss-cross all the way down. Tie and knot the cord again at the base. Bind the stick quite tightly so that the sprigs don't fall out.

4 Trim the bound stick at the top and at the base, using sharp scissors or a knife with a serrated edge. Discard the offcuts and store your sticks in a cool, dry place, away from direct sunlight. When using a lit stick, always hold a saucer or small bowl under it as you walk around the room to catch any glowing embers.

The smudging ceremony

Smudging is one of the strongest cleansing ceremonies to perform, because the herbal smoke removes old energy, even if it has been deeply embedded in the walls for many years. It can also shift unwanted predecessor energy left by a property's previous occupants, so this is a good ritual to use when you first move into a new home.

Smudging after clutter-clearing will completely change the ambience of your rooms – the musty energy will be blown away forever, leaving a feeling of balance and harmony once more.

Before you start smudging, it can be beneficial to meditate for a few minutes to clear your busy brain and connect to your inner self. Then move around the room, letting your intuition guide you. If you feel drawn to linger in a particular space, waft more smoke into the area and then move on.

If you use a feather, shake it briskly at the end of the smudging ceremony in order to discharge its energy. Then put it away until it is needed again.

Safe smudging
Smudge sticks smolder rather than burn brightly, and emit glowing embers that can damage rugs and soft furnishings. Use a saucer or a heatproof dish to catch any ash and embers that fall as you smudge each room.

USING A SMUDGE STICK

Change into some casual clothes and wash your hands before you start.

1 Mentally ask your spirit guide to get rid of any emotional upsets and then establish the intent of your cleansing ritual. Light your smudge stick and leave it burning for a few minutes, fanning the flames until it is smoldering well. Blow out the flames and let it smoke.

2 Try to connect to the spirit of your home, saying why you are doing the cleansing. Now walk clockwise around the room from the door, holding the smoldering smudge stick over a fireproof dish. Waft the smoke, with your hand or with a feather, into every corner. Keep mentally repeating your intent as you work slowly through the room.

3 When you have finished, hold the stick under cold running water to put it out. Cut off the burned bit and store the rest for further use. Open all the doors and windows.

4 If the energy is very heavy, repeat the technique for two or three days, and then do it once more the following week. Repeat the ceremony in all the rooms that need purifying.

Because the smudging smoke tends to get in you hair and clothes, when you have finished the ceremony you may need to launder the clothes you have been wearing and take another shower.

Dissipating the smoke
Use the back of you hand to waft the smoke into deep corners to dispel stagnant energy.

CLEANSING AFTER AN ARGUMENT

After an argument in your home, you need to remove the negative vibrations that still remain. Light your smudge stick, letting it smolder well before putting out the flames. Holding the stick, first waft the smoke all around yourself, and then around the affected room into all the corners, asking for all the bad feelings to be taken away. Even if you were in the right, send loving feelings and forgiveness from your heart chakra to the person with whom you argued; you will feel transformed. Now open all the windows and light a couple of candles to bring in fresh, positive energy.

Salt Cleansing

Salt is a traditional cleanser that has been part of purification ceremonies for many centuries in cultures throughout the world. The Christian use of salt is thought to have been inherited from the Romans, who traditionally used salt to banish negativity. In parts of Egypt the floors of the home are covered with salt at the start of the month-long festival of Ramadan, when Muslims purify themselves by fasting from sunrise to sunset.

What makes salt an important tool for purification is its strong antiseptic healing qualities. The best type of salt to use in rituals is either rock or sea salt. The differences between the two are minor, but sea salt brings the influences of the sea, which are thought to help with clearing out and with emotional healing. Rock salt, on the other hand, has earthly power and is believed to bring a feeling of being grounded and balanced. If you want to grind

A handful of healing
Sea salt and rock salt act like tiny crystals. Together they form a mini energy-mountain that shifts negative energy. Salt purifies the atmosphere and absorbs negative vibrations; traditionally, it is sprinkled in a small pile in a dish, or into a line or circle in rooms.

your own salt, you can use a pestle and mortar to produce very fine salt crystals.

Salt will clear energy well on its own, but when a deep cleansing is needed, it may be combined with smudging (see pages 58–61), aromatherapy (see pages 68–71), or ceremonies using sound (see pages 72–85). Once the salt is sprinkled in a room, it immediately begins to absorb any impurities that exist there.

SPRINKLING THE SALT

If you like, you can grind your chosen salt until it is very fine, so that it can more easily soak up stagnant energies. The power of salt lies in its crystalline structure, which helps to channel positive energy in our homes.

1 Put your salt in a bowl, then hold it for a few minutes to make your connection with it and set the intent for your cleansing.

2 Sprinkle a line of salt across the threshold. Then move clockwise around the room, lining the perimeter.

3 Sprinkle a pile of salt into each corner, and leave a pile in the middle of the room (you can also put this in bowls) for deeper purifying. Leave it for 24 hours and then vacuum it up. Leave a little salt in the corners as these areas get stagnant more quickly. Repeat the process in all the rooms that require cleansing.

Purifying corners

Place a small pile of salt crystals on a mat or in a dish in each corner in a room to promote cleansing and healing.

PROTECTING YOUR SLEEP

Salt is a great protector, so if you are experiencing bad dreams, or having a difficult time at work or within any kind of personal relationship, you can use some in the bedroom to protect you against such upsets. Sprinkle a thick ring of sea or rock salt around your bed and place some more in a bowl next to it (remember to renew the salt every two to three days). You are at your most vulnerable when you are asleep in bed, but your salt circle will keep you safe, helping you to let go of the negative influences of the day and to wake up feeling refreshed the next morning.

Using Incense and Candles

Incense sticks are burned in temples throughout the Far East, creating a wonderful sweet, fragrant fog that purifies the air for the many worshippers who go there to make offerings to their gods. The powerful aroma – which derives from fragrant plant oils, resins, and powders – affects mood, increases concentration, and helps people to relax and pray or meditate more easily.

Sticks, cones, and coils of incense are available, and lighting them in the home is a simple way of clearing and lifting negative vibrations. The burning incense smoke cannot cleanse as strongly as smudge sticks or aromatherapy oils, so to remove very stagnant energy in your home it is best to use them in conjunction with these other methods.

Incense boxes

To use an incense box, place the incense stick inside with its end protruding outside. As the lit stick burns, the smoke seeps through the holes in the wood, scenting the air and the wood itself.

Using incense

Always buy a good-quality brand of incense, and choose the fragrance that seems right for your intention (see chart). Buy combustible forms (sticks, cones, or coils) that will burn continuously once lit. It is a good idea to have several fragrances to hand, because one may seem more appropriate than another for the ceremony you wish to perform.

When incense is burning it gets very hot, so place it over a fireproof container. Wood or ceramic holders support the stick of incense and have a groove to catch the ash as it falls off.

Place the stick or cone of incense in its holder, and light the tip. When it is glowing, blow out the flame so that it starts to smoke. Set the intent for your purification ceremony. Leave the incense on a shelf or table, or waft it around the room. Repeat in other rooms.

CLEANSING YOUR AURA

If you are feeling down, or somebody has upset you, do this short aura cleansing ceremony. Choose from rose, vanilla, clove, orange, or lemon incense. Light the stick as described above; when it is smoking well, close your eyes and ask your spirit guide to help cleanse you. Waft the smoke down your right side, up over your head, and down your left side. Bring the smoke down the front of your body, let it linger by your heart, then waft it down your back toward the ground. Visualize anger, sadness, or upset dissipating into the smoke as you become balanced once more.

CHOOSING INCENSE

Many different fragrances are available, so choose about three that really appeal to you. Let your senses lead you, because the sense of smell is very personal, but bear in mind the purification process for which you need it.

FRAGRANCE	USES
Basil	Can help to harmonize the atmosphere in the home, increasing the empathy of people living there
Bergamot	Provides some spiritual protection, and is believed to increase prosperity
Cedarwood	Improves feelings of security and safety
Cinnamon	Can counteract illness and boost feelings of conviviality
Cypress	Eases depression for those who are mourning
Frankincense	Soothes the nerves and is very spiritually uplifting
Jasmine	Reduces anxiety and helps meditation
Lavender	Is relaxing, calming, and soothing
Myrrh	Is very emotionally grounding
Patchouli	Promotes sensuality and a cheerful, peaceful atmosphere
Rose	Encourages warm, loving feelings
Sandalwood	Very effective in clearing space; also enhances meditation

PURITY POINT 94

♦ Put an unlit stick of incense in your car to freshen the air.

Candles

Candles are wonderful energizers, which have a long religious history: temples and churches have the uplifting glow of candles in them, and visitors will often light a candle to dedicate to a loved, deceased relative. In the home the positive, yang energy of candles will revitalize a room's atmosphere. However, as with incense, for an intensive purifying ceremony they are best combined with another technique such as drumming or using a singing bowl (see pages 80–83, 76–79).

USING CANDLES

Candles are widely available in many different shapes, colors, and sizes. Choose a color that you think works with your ceremony (see chart), and ideally buy ones that are scented with essential oils, which will strengthen the candles' cleansing and uplifting properties.

Place the candles for your cleansing ritual in holders to catch the wax, and never leave them unattended when they are lit.

Light candles in all the rooms you are clearing, mentally stating your intent for the purification ceremony that you want them to perform.

Gaze into the flames for a few minutes, feeling how the room's energy is already starting to change for the better, bringing in light and warmth.

Candle etiquette
In some cultures candles are never blown out, in order to respect the Fire spirits, so use a candle snuffer or carefully pinch out the flame instead.

INCREASING YOUR CREATIVITY

To increase your concentration and creative thoughts, burn two or three stimulating yellow candles in your home office. Before you light them, hold them for a few moments, stating what projects you need help with. Light the candles and feel the positive thought patterns engulfing you.

CHOOSING CANDLES

You can bring in some basic color therapy when choosing the candles to use in your clearing ritual. The warmer or cooler vibrations of the various colors will create a different feel to the room being cleansed; choose one that achieves the effect you desire.

Candle colors
Candle colors link to your aspirations.

COLOR	GENERAL EFFECTS
Red	A warm stimulating color that encourages physical activity; it can also revive passion in the bedroom
Orange	A creative color to enliven a room and bring in joy and enthusiasm
Cinnamon/ light brown	A stable, grounding color that will harmonize a room
Yellow	A mentally stimulating color that can help arouse lively conversations or increase concentration
Green	A harmonizing color that brings balance, soothes the emotions, and offers security and protection
Blue	A calm, cool color that engenders feelings of peace, particularly in the bedroom
Purple	A soothing, intuitive, and psychic color, used for cleansing meditation rooms and bedrooms
White	The color of purity; it gives protection and comfort
Gold	The color of abundance and understanding; it can counteract a lack of interest in life
Silver	The color of the moon; a balancing color that encourages change and learning

Pure Aromatherapy

The healing properties of plants have been used for centuries by numerous cultures. More than 2,000 years ago Hippocrates, the Greek father of medicine, spoke of the healing benefits of aromatic scents in baths and oils. It was also recognized early on that burning plants or their oils produced a variety of sensory effects, such as feelings of wellbeing, calm, or a healing aroma for the sick. The essential oils used in aromatherapy are distilled from herbs and other plants; their scents give out the spirit and energy of the plant from which they are extracted. In the home essential oils can instantly influence the atmosphere, inducing vibrancy or a feeling of calm.

CLEARING THE ATMOSPHERE

Some oils also have deep cleansing properties that can get rid of any stale energy that is left in the home after de-cluttering. Lavender is a versatile oil that has the same vibration as neutral chi so it can shift any stubborn energy, such as predecessor energy left by former occupants, which is lingering in the home. For general cleansing juniper, sage, pine, or eucalyptus oils are ideal. Citrus oils, such as lemon, lime, or orange are very revitalizing, adding a fresh stimulus to a room's ambience.

BUYING OILS

Essential oils are readily available in health stores, and act more effectively than synthetic products to change the energy vibrations in your home. Always buy a well-known make, so that you know that each bottle you choose contains the true spiritual essence of the plants from which it was distilled; avoid cheaper synthetic scents or oils that are blended with a vegetable oil, because they do not have the same effect.

Healing herbs
Herbs have been used for centuries for their therapeutic healing properties. Many types of essential oils are distilled from plants, flowers, trees, and bark.

CHOOSING OILS

Decide on the type of purification you need, then select the right essential oil for your ceremony. There are many oils to choose from, so only the ones with the best cleansing properties are included here. Check the scent of the oils to which you feel drawn, because there will probably be one that appeals to you more than the rest. Some oils also work well for a daily uplift.

ESSENTIAL OIL	QUALITIES
Chamomile	A calming oil that is good for clearing away bad vibrations after an upset or argument
Eucalyptus	An invigorating and cleansing oil
Geranium	A harmonizing oil that lifts depression and stabilizes the emotions; mixed with lavender, it creates a calm atmosphere
Juniper	An oil renowned for its stimulating, purifying, and protective properties
Lavender	A soothing oil that cleanses deeply, returning energy (chi) to a neutral state
Lemon	A refreshing oil that is mentally stimulating
Lime	An invigorating oil that lifts the spirits
Orange	A balancing oil that enlivens the home; good for cleansing the atmosphere of animal smells
Pine	A tangy oil that cleanses deeply
Sage	A oil with special purifying properties
Sandalwood	A sacred oil in the East; it reduces stress, soothes anxiety, and releases fear
Tea tree	An antiseptic oil that brings healing and cleanses a sick room

Chamomile flowers

Lavender seeds

Lemon verbena and orange

The aromatherapy ceremony

Misting with essential oils is a pleasant way to shift energy levels, because you are left with a delicious, natural fragrance in every room of your home. Many essential oils have powerful purifying properties that can move the stale energy that is left in rooms after you have cleared out piles of old possessions. Choose an oil from the chart on page 69 to suit the depth of cleansing that you think you need.

Geranium essential oil, for example, has a wonderful scent and can lift the atmosphere after an emotional upset. If you are trying to restore harmony after a stressful time,

sandalwood essential oil is a potent balancing oil. If a family member has been ill recently, you can mist their bedroom and the rest of the home to energize and promote healing. Once you have misted, you will immediately feel better and will notice a positive change in the vibrancy of your home. Misting is so easy to perform that you can quickly make it a part of your regular domestic routine.

Fragrant scents
Aromatherapy oils, also known as essential oils, evoke the unique perfumes of the plants and flowers from which they are distilled.

MISTING WITH ESSENTIAL OILS

If you want to mist regularly, change your chosen oil every few days, because plastic misters can affect an oil's properties. Alternatively, store the mixture for one to two weeks in a dark glass atomizer.

1 Fill a mister bottle with water, add a few drops of your chosen oil, and shake well. First cleanse your aura with oils (see page 56), then stand still for a moment, close your eyes, and set your purifying intent for the ceremony. Say it out loud, if you prefer, to reaffirm it. Really connect with your home as you do this.

2 Starting at the door of the room you are purifying, walk round it clockwise, spraying all around, not forgetting the dark corners. Repeat in all the other rooms that need cleansing.

3 If the energy has felt very heavy, repeat the misting every day for a week. Then do it weekly as a top-up. If you decide to use lavender oil, try to spray every room daily for 28 days, as this represents a cycle of chi.

Misting
A misting solution consists of a few drops of aromatherapy essential oil added to water. You can use glass or plastic mister bottles.

REVIVING ROMANCE IN THE BEDROOM

If you feel that your love life with your partner has deteriorated, do a short ceremony in your bedroom to increase the loving emanations that exist there. Use some jasmine or patchouli oil, because these heavy, seductive scents are best for the bedroom since they are similar to your own natural body smell. Place a few drops in a mister bottle filled with water. Spray around your bedroom, saying mentally in your head how you want your love life to improve. Mist over your bed and pillows so that the sensual aroma lingers there. To finish, light two red candles for a short while to give a final romantic boost to your boudoir.

Using Sound

When you purify a room using sound, any of the following techniques work well. You can even try improvising with your own "instrument", such as a saucepan. Sound has energy; it is a strong vibration that can cleanse and shift any sluggish or stagnant energy that exists in your home. It doesn't matter which tool you choose so much as the intention you impart as you are doing your purifying. As you use your hands, voice or instrument, feel a shift in your consciousness as you become part of the sound. Sense its high vibrations moving inside you, which then flow out of you and fill the room. As the sounds radiate directly from you, see how every sound in the room starts to harmonize and come into balance, creating a place that literally glows with energy.

Clapping

This is a very easy, but extremely effective, method for shifting stale energies. Think back to when you were last at a large concert and how the atmosphere was almost electric at the end when hundreds of people were clapping for an encore.

Clapping up the energy at home will bring about a serious shift, but if you are feeling very dragged down by an extremely heavy energy permeating your home and feel in need of an intense space clearing, combine it with smudging, aromatherapy, or drumming (see pages 58–61, 68–71 and 80–83).

Big claps
Start with large, loud claps, holding your hands further apart to shift the dull energy in a room.

PURITY POINT 95

♦ Always wash your hands under a running tap after clapping to remove any negative energy that is clinging to you.

THE CLAPPING TECHNIQUE

You can use this method anywhere for a quick uplift, even in a hotel room when traveling, if you don't feel happy with its atmosphere. Try out some short, fast claps at your first corner before you start to see how it feels and to sense the room's energy.

1 Relax your body and slightly bend your knees. To test the energy, do some small fast claps and see how they sound. If they are muffled, clap harder to disperse the stagnancy.

2 Stand at the door of the room silently for a few moments, and set your purifying intent, concentrating on really connecting with your home. Hold the thought in your mind as you walk clockwise round the room using large, louder claps.

3 Intensify the speed of your clapping in corners as energy really gets stuck here, moving up and down the wall. The clapping should sound very crisp and clear. If there are areas where it is very dull, clap from the floor up to the ceiling to raise the energy. Clap in cupboards if you want. Repeat this process in all the rooms that need clearing.

Small claps
Doing small, frequent claps quickly creates more positive energy, particularly in corners where it tends to be stale and slow.

ENERGIZING AN OFFICE

Clapping is the ideal medium to improve the energy in an office room before an important meeting with clients or other members of staff. If you are not happy with the feel of the room it will not encourage a happy conclusion to your discussions. Pause in the doorway and think what you want to achieve from the meeting. Holding that thought in your mind, clap all the way round the room, concentrating on louder claps over the chairs and above the conference table. When you have finished, open the windows to blow away the negative fall-out.

Ringing bells

Bells give out a wonderful clear sound, which is believed by many spiritual people to resonate far out into the universe. They have long had a religious connection in Asia, and in parts of Europe people are still woken on a Sunday morning to clear chiming church bells calling the faithful to their morning service.

When bells are used for space clearing they can dislodge stuck energy that it is hard to shift with techniques such as clapping. The clear energy sound field that is left will resonate in your home for a long time to come.

The right bell
A decorative temple bell bought in the East can be a cherished possession, but a simple ringing bell is just as effective for a purification ceremony.

BUYING BELLS

If you want to use bells regularly, aim to buy a series from a specialist music shop that are the same shape, varying from small to large (1–4 in [2.5 cm–10 cm]). The larger bells break up the heavy energy, while the smaller bells do the final purifying. Choose a bell that appeals to you. When you really love a bell, it can develop a special energy that will clear your home very quickly. Versatile Tibetan bells are generally made from seven metals; brass bells give an unpredictable sound, but generate a

USING A BELL

Ideally only ring your bell yourself, or lend it to people you trust, to keep the vibrations positive. When you unwrap your bell (each bell if using a set), hold it briefly in your hands to tune into it. Go to the middle of the room and ring or strike the bell. If it sounds muffled the energy is very stagnant.

1 Pause in the door of the room, close your eyes and focus on your purification intent and getting in tune with your home. Walk clockwise round the room ringing the bell from the floor up towards the ceiling, and in corners, to shift the energy. The sound should become clearer and stronger. If it still sounds muffled in certain places, keep ringing the bell until the sound changes.

2 Repeat ringing round the room with the smaller bells until you have a crystal clear sound. Finally, stop the ringing bell with your hand. Repeat in other rooms that need clearing.

REVITALIZING YOUR CAR

If it is hard to concentrate while driving in your car, or if you have had several minor accidents, cleansing it with a bell will improve its atmosphere. Use a small bell, and sit holding it in the car for a few moments concentrating on the task ahead. Then ring all round the front seats and then round the back. Repeat two or three times until you achieve a really clear sound.

yang energy, while bronze bells can have a grounding effect. Brass and gold Balinese temple bells are made to ring with a wonderful clear sound. Store your bell or bells, wrapped in cloth, in a special place, high up on a shelf.

Ringing a bell

Swinging a bell back and forth creates motion and sound together. The clear resonance of a bell lifts the energy of a room as it gets louder and stronger.

Striking a bell

If you prefer, you can strike a large bell with a wooden mallet to create a positive ringing tone.

PURITY POINT 96

♦ Open a window while ringing a bell to let the stagnancy flow away.

Singing bowls

In the West singing bowls are relatively new, having only become available in the 1960s. But in the East their uses for meditation or healing have been known for thousands of years. The spiritual homeland of singing bowls is Tibet, but the Tibetans were versatile traders and it is believed that the bowls may have originated elsewhere, because ancient singing bowls have also been discovered in India, Nepal, and Japan. They have been in existence for around 4,000 years. Excavations in 1938 of a Tibetan temple, which was dated to around 2400 B.C.E, discovered two singing bowls buried in the ruins. The temple belonged to the ancient animistic Bon religion, which pre-dates Buddhism.

Tapping a bowl
You can also choose to strike the bowl using the mallet, rather than use circular motions to create a rhythmic sound. This technique can be particularly helpful when clearing areas where the energy is proving difficult to shift.

Hand-made bowls
Hand-beaten singing bowls can give the best resonance.

MEDITATING WITH YOUR BOWL

First, light a candle. This will act as a focus for your meditation. Sit cross-legged on a cushion on the floor, and hold the bowl lovingly in your hands. Take a few deep breaths, then stroke the metal bowl with its wooden mallet on the inner or outer rim to create its unique sound. As the vibration builds, feel it relaxing you as you gaze steadily into the candle flame. Let all the negative thoughts of the day drift from your mind, until you find you are thinking of nothing at all. After about 5–10 minutes, slowly stop playing your bowl and come back to reality. Snuff out the candle.

In the past the use of singing bowls was shrouded in mystery, even in Tibet, but that changed when many monks left the country during the early 1950s after China took over the country. Living in northern India and Nepal, they sold their singing bowls in order to pay for food, and in this way the wonderful versatility of these instruments finally became known to other people.

CHOOSING A BOWL

Singing bowls are wonderful instruments to lift the atmosphere in a room, and can quickly raise the energy after an argument or major clear-out, or make you feel better if you are feeling down. Today they are normally made in Nepal or Tibet, and are lovingly crafted, either by hand or machine, from around seven different metals, one of which is often a precious metal such as platinum, gold, or silver. There are also bowls made from clear quartz, although these are more fragile to use and usually more difficult to find than the traditional metal singing bowls.

When you buy a singing bowl from a store, try different ones until you find a tone that really lifts your spirit. Just slightly dampening the wooden mallet that plays the bowl can change the overall tone, so experiment. The sound produced by the bowl creates a wonderful energy field that clears out negativity; unusually, it also helps to draw in new, positive energy.

Bowl sizes
Singing bowls come in a huge array of sizes and types, from 2 in (5 cm) diameter to 10 in (25 cm) diameter and above.

The singing bowl ceremony

The wonderful humming sound of singing bowls is an effective energizer. When you stroke the bowl firmly with the wooden mallet, the spinning sound that emanates from it expands outward in ever-increasing circles, and also spirals back down into the middle of the bowl. As the circles gradually expand, they whirl away any negative and stagnant energy that exists within the room.

BALANCING YOUR CHAKRAS

Your singing bowl can also be used to harmonize your chakras (your spiritual energy centers), particularly when you are feeling down or depressed. There are seven principal body chakras, and each is associated with a color (see right). Sit cross-legged on a mat or in an upright chair, holding your bowl, then start to build up the sound following the steps given above. As the vibrations get stronger, close your eyes and take several deep breaths to relax you. Then focus for a couple of minutes on each chakra, feeling the positive sound energy filling you. First focus on your root chakra, in your lower spine and pelvic area; then move on to your sacral chakra, just below your navel; up to the solar plexus chakra, just below your breastbone; and then to the heart chakra, in your upper chest. Feel the energy filling all these chakras, before flowing upward to your throat chakra, then your "third eye" in the middle of your forehead, and finally your crown chakra on top of your head. Slowly let the humming of your bowl stop, open your eyes, and notice how much better you feel.

CHAKRA COLORS

Each of the seven chakras links with a color that you can visualize as you do the chakra exercise.

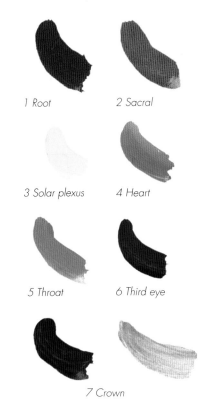

1 Root   *2 Sacral*

3 Solar plexus   *4 Heart*

5 Throat   *6 Third eye*

7 Crown

USING A SINGING BOWL

Always stand in the middle of the room to be cleared as the bowl must be stationary to reach maximum volume. When you start to play your singing bowl, take some time to build up the clear tone. Feel yourself becoming part of the sound as the bowl's vibrations expand and get louder, reverberating throughout the room.

Before you begin, hold your bowl in your hands for a few minutes to make a connection with it. Close your eyes and set your intent of what you want it to achieve for you. You can also place your bowl on a cushion or other soft surface.

1 Place the bowl in the flat palm of one hand, and take the mallet and start moving it around the inner or outer edge of the bowl, and feel the sound start to build up.

2 Move the mallet faster, feeling the bowl's singing energy spiral around you. Sense negative energy whirling away and brighter energy being pulled in. Slowly stop playing the bowl; repeat in other rooms as needed.

Rhythmic drumming

From ancient times people throughout the world have featured the drum in cultural rituals, healing, and religious ceremonies. Different drumming rhythms have stimulated or calmed the emotions, or helped people make connections with the subconscious mind. To Native Americans the drumbeat has a sacred symbolism, for they believe it represents the heartbeat of Mother Earth.

In many traditional cultures the sound of the drum is used by the shaman, or medicine man, to clear congested energy. The consistent drumming rhythm alters his brainwave patterns, putting him in a trance or altered state of consciousness, where he may receive guidance from the spirits while he is clearing a room. As he concentrates on the drum beat, he connects to other mind levels or realities that cannot normally be reached. The rhythmic beating of the drum seems to create a bridge to these other states of consciousness.

The other reason why drums are favored by shamans for space clearing is because the vibrations from the drum are so strong that they quickly shift a negative atmosphere and encourage free-flowing energy once more.

Types of drum
The drum shown right is an African Djembe drum, made from hollowed wood. It gives a deep, round sound. Drums made from clay can have a tighter, more shallow resonance.

BUYING A DRUM

Drums are available from specialist instrument stores. They are made from different materials, but the most common type has an animal-skin membrane stretched over a wooden frame or base. For purifying a room the most popular version is a hand-held drum, with an animal skin stretched over a circular wooden hoop. However, any kind of drum works to clear the atmosphere, so search for one that you like the sound of and which looks appealing to you.

Drumming techniques

Some drums, such as the Turkish drum (known as a Dooblek) are played from the side rather than between the knees. This works well if you feel you want to walk around rooms to clear negative energy there, but some people may find this drumming position less comfortable than resting the drum between the knees.

INCREASING YOUR SELF-ESTEEM

If you have lost confidence in yourself, try this simple ritual to build your self-esteem. Sit on a large cushion on the floor, holding your drum loosely between your knees, honoring this special instrument. Close your eyes and start a slow two-beat rhythm on it with your hands, imitating the steady beat of your heart. Feel your mind being lost in the hypnotic sound. As you start to drift, reproduce in your mind a situation where you have felt supremely happy – enjoying a holiday, being praised at work, or experiencing the thrill of receiving an award. Bask in the glory of this sensation and see how good it makes you feel. Notice how any anxiety about your self-worth just floats away. Slowly come to and open your eyes. Whenever you feel down, repeat the exercise.

PURITY POINT 98

♦ If you are drumming on a wet day, slightly warm a membrane made of animal skin under a lamp. Conversely, on a hot day lightly mist the skin.

Drumming to clear energy

The drum is a very powerful instrument in space clearing, particularly if you are trying to remove heavy emotional debris, predecessor energy, or if you have had a major clutter-busting session. As you beat the drum, the musty energy in your room changes structure, and you balance the male and female energies in yourself and your home. By doing this, you also harmonize the forces of yin (feminine) and yang (masculine).

When your drum is not in use, hang it in a special place; treat it with respect, and never be tempted to use it as an additional surface for keeping any items on. If you travel with it, buy a protective bag to keep it in.

Every drum you use has its own personality and sound. As you pick up different drums you will notice the change. Some have a softer,

Hand drum
Small hand drums beat when they are rotated by your hands. They are usually lightweight, and are easy to carry around when performing a purification ritual.

more reserved sound, while others are louder and more vibrant.

Some cultures believe that drums are either masculine or feminine, and that they display the characteristics of their genders when they are played. When you drum, you may feel that time has stopped and you can lose yourself in the compelling rhythm, letting any thoughts about your life now, in the past or future, filter past you.

FREEING EMOTIONAL ENERGY

When there has been a serious illness or death in the home, the sweet, sickly emanations that still fester need to be removed. Sit with your drum in the affected room. Close your eyes and concentrate on releasing the spirit of the person who has gone, or mentally celebrate the recovery of the one who was sick. Start drumming slowly and relish how you become part of the rhythm. Feel the vibrancy slowly returning to the room. Finish drumming when the time seems right. Hold your drum to your heart for a short time, then open a window to blow away any remaining vibrations of sadness or ill health.

USING A DRUM

Before you start drumming, hold your drum close to your body. Run your fingers over its surface and frame, so that you make a strong connection to it. Try out a few drumbeats with your hands, keeping your wrists loose and letting the movement come from them, not from your arms.

1 Sit in the middle of the room to be cleansed. Relax and close your eyes. Sense your home around you, and mentally set your intent for the cleansing. Start drumming with a very primal two-beat rhythm. Allow your body to relax – the drum will let you know what beat is required. Sense how your heartbeat seems to synchronize with the drumbeat.

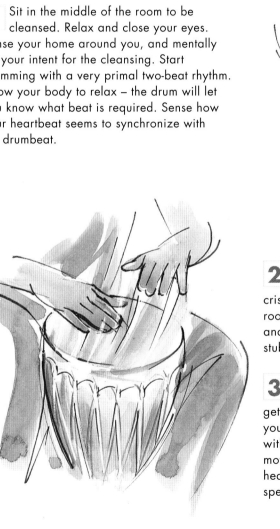

2 Feel how the energy starts to lift after a short time and how your drumbeats get crisper and clearer. Move to each corner of the room, starting at the left and circling around, and drum faster in the corners to disperse stubborn, sticky energy.

3 When you are ready to move on to other rooms, you may find that your drumbeats get faster or slower; trust your intuition to tell you what is needed. When you are happy with the room's atmosphere, stop drumming, move your drum in a circle, and hold it to your heart briefly. Drum in all the rooms that need a special uplift.

Chanting, toning, and singing

Using your voice is a pleasant way of working with sound to create an energy shift. The three techniques will not shift heavy energy, but are great for giving a general uplift. The volume and sound that you create with your voice activates the energy flow, it also awakens your consciousness and feeds your spirituality.

PURITY POINT 99

♦ Spend some time speaking or singing the sounds to give you more power for your clearing ceremony.

Mantras

The famous mantra of peace and harmony is *Om mani padme hum*, shown here in Sanskrit. It means, "Hail, the jewel in the lotus".

CHANTING

Monks have used chanting for years as a community activity and to aid their spiritual wellbeing. The sounds that were created in Latin changes such as "gloria in excelsis deo" fuelled their spiritual and emotional wellbeing. It was found that if the monks didn't chant they became tired and depressed. Chanting is easy, you find a mantra that appeals to you and chant it continuously. Most mantras are in

ॐ मणि पद्मे हुं

| om | mani | padme | hum |

hail the jewel in the lotus

FINDING INNER PEACE

If you are very stressed, do this small ceremony to connect with your inner consciousness. Light some candles, and sit cross-legged on a cushion on the floor. Start chanting or toning and feel the sound travel from deep inside you and out into the room. Sense how every body cell is vibrating and how your worries are released into the atmosphere. Keep the sound going for 5–10 minutes, then slowly stop and come to, relishing how calm you feel.

Prayer beads
Use mala beads (Buddhist prayer beads) or a rosary to count your mantras.

Sanskrit, an ancient Indian language – the most famous of which is "Om" (see the illustration, left). You can also chant with words such as "love" or "peace", but it is often better to chant in a foreign language because our own words can have too many associations.

TONING

Toning is believed to be an ancient method of healing that restores people's minds and bodies to their normal harmonic pattern.

Toning is easy to do – you consciously hold one note, a sound, for a long time. It is a process where making vocal sounds creates balance and stimulates energy flow. One way of toning is to use the vowel sounds: "oh", "ah", "eh", and "eee", keeping your jaw loose and free as you say them. See how the sounds resonate from different parts of your body and on your spiritual centers, the chakras, and the strong effect that they have on the room that you are cleansing.

USING CHANTS, TONES, AND SONGS

Choose the method that appeals to you to do your ceremony. Let the sound come from deep in your body and feel its strength.

1 Stand in the doorway of the room, close your eyes and set your purifying intent. Start chanting, toning, or singing as you walk clockwise around the room.

2 Feel the strength of the sound coming from you as you walk several times around the room. When you hear a tone change, stay for a few moments until a clearer sound comes through. Keep walking round until you hear a crisp, clear sound in every part of the room. Repeat in all the rooms that need clearing.

SINGING

When you sing a favorite song, have you noticed how any depressed feelings you are experiencing just disappear? Singing has such a powerful vibration that high notes can even break glass. Sing a song that fills you with joy and this emotion will be reflected back into the room.

Water Cleansing

A ritual cleanser since early times, water is still revered by Christians in the ceremony known as baptism. Adults were once fully immersed in water to purify them in this special rebirth ritual. Today it is normally babies who are baptized, and they are cleansed by being sprinkled with water from the church font.

Water is a simple tool for cleansing the home, but it does have the ability to remove negative energy and bring about peace and clarity. As water is also linked to the emotions, it has a certain potency for dispersing bitterness or anxiety – for example, after an emotional outburst in a room. For a major boost after clearing out masses of clutter you may want to combine water purifying with smudging (see page 58–61), aromatherapy (see pages 68–71), or drumming (see pages 80–83).

Water energizer
A simple purifier, water can dispel negative energy that exists in the home. To continue the cleansing process, leave a bowl of water out after your purification ceremony.

PREPARING WATER

Before you do your water ceremony, you need to energize the water that you are using. Fill a glass bowl with water from the faucet, then charge it in one of two ways:

Charging with sunlight Place the bowl outside on a sunny window ledge and leave for about three hours, so that the sun's rays energize it.

Charging with a quartz crystal Take a large piece of natural quartz crystal. First, cleanse it for 24 hours by placing it in a small bowl or jar of water to remove other energies from the stone. Then put it in your bowl of water. Leave the crystal for 24 hours to allow the intrinsic energizing vibrations of the crystal to pass into the water.

USING WATER

1 To do your water ceremony, it is good to follow an old shamanic tradition, where the charged water is flicked around the room with a healing herb sprig, such as rosemary, lavender, or marjoram.

2 Take your bowl of charged water and hold it to you for a few moments. Close your eyes, feel the water's innate power, and set your intent for clearing the energy.

3 Walk clockwise from the door around the room, flicking water with your herb sprig as you go, and sprinkling more water as necessary into dull corners.

4 Follow your senses – if part of the room seems very clogged, stand still and flick some more water into this spot for a few minutes. Repeat the process in all the other rooms that need cleansing.

MISTING A ROOM AFTER AN UPSET

To give instant healing to a room when an emotional outburst has occurred, mist it with some charged water. Pour the water into a mister, then hold it for a few minutes, mentally imagining how you want to clear the emotional fallout. Then mist all around the room and feel how the anger and sadness are dispersed. As you spray, negative ions (ironically, positive ions are not actually good for you) are released into the air, making it healthier. Sense how the room feels revitalized and inspiring once more.

Healing water
You can use a sprig of lavender or other woody herb such as thyme or rosemary for water cleansing. Flick the water around the room, making sure it gets into dark, stale corners.

Creating Your Own Purification Ceremonies

Once you have mastered the basic purification techniques, you can enjoy personalizing your own ceremonies to bring in the changes you need. Focus on what you desire, or on what requires change, and believe completely in the outcome of your ceremony. As you purify and energize the atmosphere, let your intention go out into the universe – whatever you ask is unlikely to be refused, unless subconsciously you do not want it to happen. Try the ceremonies described on the next few pages, or adapt the methods to your own needs.

For these ceremonies you do not need to follow all the purification tips on page 57, but it is a good is to take a bath or shower first and to cleanse your aura with a burning incense stick. Remove jewelry, unplug the phone, and choose a time when you will not be disturbed.

Harnessing earth energy

Glass, pebbles, and crystals all strengthen the Earth element and can also help to attract love.

ATTRACTING A NEW LOVER CEREMONY

If you have been single for a while and would like to bring in a new partner, do this ceremony to clear out any vibrations that may be holding you back or linking you to a past love.

WHAT YOU NEED:

♦ A recent photo of your past love (if relevant) and a saucer or bowl

♦ Cones or sticks of a favorite incense (or ones using rose and jasmine)

♦ A picture of a symbolic attractive partner, or a photo of your desired lover

♦ A picture frame

♦ A red box and a rose-quartz crystal

♦ One or two red candles, and paper and pen

Love altar
You can search for a picture of your symbolic ideal partner from a periodical or advertising literature.

1 Make a special altar for your ceremony on a table in the Marriage and Romantic Happiness area in the southwest of your bedroom or living room. If you have a past love whom you haven't totally let go of, tear up their photo and place the pieces in a saucer or bowl on the altar. Surround it with incense cones, or place incense sticks nearby. Put your symbolic or real picture in the frame and set it next to the saucer.

2 Write down on a piece of paper the main qualities that you want in your new lover, then place your list in the red box along with the rose quartz crystal (the lover's stone). Light the candles and incense.

3 As the incense circulates, sit before your altar and visualize your past love, or any negative feelings, disappearing into the smoke. Look at your symbolic or real picture and concentrate on pulling in a new lover with your desired qualities.

4 Sit for several minutes, concentrating on this intent, then blow out the incense and the candles. Leave the altar for one week, and the red box, until you start a new relationship. Burn the candles regularly to fire up your love energy.

BRINGING IN WEALTH AND PROSPERITY CEREMONY

This short, uplifting ceremony. will help to remove any negativity that is stopping your income from florishing.

WHAT YOU NEED:

♦ A bowl of coins to encourage wealth

♦ Your check book and bank statements

♦ A purse/wallet

♦ A bowl of water with pebbles to energize

♦ A sweetgrass smudge stick and fireproof dish

1 Place all your financial items and the bowl of pebbles in your Wealth and Prosperity area in the southeast corner of your living room, or on a table in the hall.

2 Light your smudge stick over a fireproof dish and, when it is well lit, blow out the flames and let it smoke. Close your eyes; concentrate on the intention for your finances to improve. Visualize yourself with a full bank account and see yourself planning how to spend your money.

3 Smudge all around the relevant corner or table, and over your check book, bank statements, and coin purse/wallet to remove any negative vibrations that are preventing you from holding onto your money.

4 Pause for a few moments to let the smudge smoke do its cleansing work, then open the

Money altar
Place a bowl of coins and your bank statements or any current savings books on your money altar.

windows for a while. Leave your items for a time to be energized, then remove them.

PURITY POINT 100

♦ If your long-term savings are performing badly, smudge all around the files that relate to these, too.

RITUAL CLEANSING CEREMONY

On a normal day we are in continual physical contact with many people, often standing shoulder to shoulder with them on trains, in buses, and in stores. We pick up their emotional vibrations, which may often be depressed, upset, or needy. So at the end of a day taking a bath with aromatherapy oils can give you the deep spiritual cleansing that you need. First shower to remove everyday grime before your ritual soaking, seeing the physical grime of the day disappearing with the soap down the drain.

WHAT YOU NEED:

♦ Lavender essential oil
♦ Geranium essential oil
♦ Several candles

1 Open a window in the bathroom to let the purifying spirit of air in, then close it and turn on the warm water to run a bath.

2 When the bath is full of water, add six to eight drops of lavender and geranium essential oil, and swirl the water around to mix them in. Place several candles on the rim of the bath, light them, and step into the water.

3 As you sink down to immerse yourself in the warmth, gaze into the flickering light of the candles and feel how any unwanted thoughts or emotions are washed completely away.

4 Stay soaking in the bath for about 15 minutes – view it as a sort of rebirth, as you visualize other people's draining energies drifting away from you in the water.

Ready for cleansing
Relaxing aromatherapy oils can be used to dispel all the emotional upsets of a working day.

PROTECTING YOUR HOME CEREMONY

Everybody wants to feel safe at home and protected from intruders. By building a spiritual force field around you, you can be secure at home and have peace of mind when you go away.

WHAT YOU NEED:

♦ Rock salt
♦ Several drops of juniper essential oil in a mister bottle or atomizer filled with water
♦ Two white candles
♦ A bell (optional)

1 Before starting your protection ritual, clean your home. Sprinkle rock salt in each doorway, then spray in a clockwise direction around each room with the juniper oil to purify stale energy and offer protection. If you have a bell, bring in extra clarity to the cleansed rooms by ringing it once in each room.

2 Sit cross-legged on a cushion in the middle of your living room with a small table in front of you, and light the candles. Sit looking into the flames, then take some deep breaths and visualize a glowing white ball of protection, which gradually gets larger and larger until it completely encircles the room. See how safe it makes you feel, then let it cover your home like a shield. Now ask the shield to allow your

Ready for protection
Salt is renowned for its protective and healing properties. In this ceremony it is used with aromatherapy misting and candles to create a sacred shield around you and your property.

friends, family, and helpers to penetrate it, but not unwanted intruders.

3 Slowly come back to the present. Vacuum up the salt within 24 hours. Repeat the ritual regularly to enforce the shield's power, or if you are going away. If you feel like extra protection, place two stone guardian animals on each side of your front door.

INCREASING YOUR FERTILITY CEREMONY

If you are thinking about having a baby, you can make a special home altar or table to encourage fertility.

WHAT YOU NEED:

♦ A happy framed picture of you and your partner

♦ A symbolic cutout picture from a periodical of a baby

♦ Russian nesting dolls

♦ Red candles

♦ A baby book with your own list of boys' and girls' names tucked inside

♦ Several drops of ylang-ylang essential oil in a mister bottle or atomizer filled with water

♦ Red tulips, or mother and child statue (optional)

Baby altar
Boost fertility by featuring baby items, red candles, you and your partner's picture, and Russian dolls.

1 Set up your altar with the first six items in your chosen place, tucking the baby picture into your framed picture. You could use your Children's area in the west of your bedroom, but in that case remove the tulips (as they are too yang here) and add the statue instead.

2 Perform the ceremony just before going to bed. Clap all around the area to clear any stagnant energy. Then spray clockwise around the room with the sensuous ylang-ylang oil, and all over your altar to encourage a special romantic atmosphere.

3 Light the candles and sit in front of your altar, gazing into the flames for several minutes and focussing on your intention to have a baby. Imagine a happy scene with your baby: bathing him, or taking her out for a walk in her pram. Remember that planting images in your subconscious mind is very powerful.

4 Slowly come to. Repeat the ritual regularly.

PURITY POINT 101

♦ If you need to do a pregnancy test, leave the box on your altar the night before you use it.

Index

Further reading

Sacred Space Denise Linn, Rider Books

Creating Sacred Space with Feng Shui Karen Kingston, Piatkus

Clearing the Clutter: 100 Ways to Energize Your Life Mary Lambert, Cico Books

The Smudge Book Jane Alexander, Element

Author's acknowledgments

I would like to thank Cindy Richards for her input on developing this book, and Liz Dean for all her usual creativity and enthusiasm in running the project. Also Sara Kidd for her attractive design and Joan Corlass, Samantha Wilson, and Moira Wills for their special artworks, and Mandy Greenfield for her sensitive editing. Finally, a special thanks to my family, particularly my sister Gill, and all my friends (a special mention to Michele, Lynne, Cathy, Sarah, and Steve) for their encouragement during the turbulent writing process.

Mary Lambert is based in London and can be contacted for feng shui and clutter-clearing consultations for homes and businesses via email: maryliz.lambert@virgin.net.

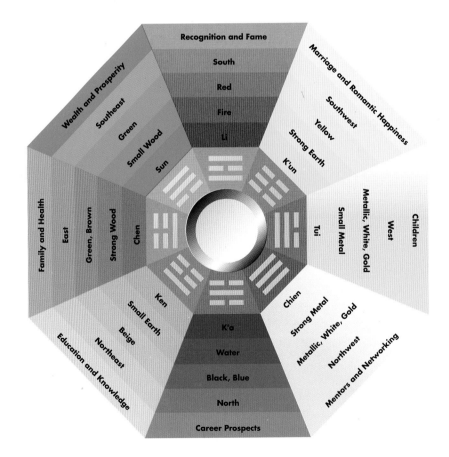